P9-CKQ-826

Etruscan

Cover Terracotta funerary urn from Chiusi, 150–100 BC. 75 × 57 × 25 cm (BM Terracotta D795. 1926.3–24.124; *CIE* 2260).

Bronze mirror with a scene from the underworld, late 4th century BC. A winged Lasa holds out a scroll inscribed with the names of the figures: Lasa, Aivas (Ajax) and Hamphiare (Amphiaraos, the Greek diviner and seer). Diam. 16.5 cm (BM Br 622, 1847.9–9.4).

Etruscan

Larissa Bonfante

University of California Press / British Museum

Acknowledgements

I am deeply grateful to the following for help, suggestions and encouragement: Vittoria and Giuliano Bonfante, Marie-Françoise Briguet, Andrew Burnett, Eirene Christodoulou, Brian Cook, Stefania Del Papa, Adriana Emiliozzi, Nancy de Grummond, Alessandro Morandi, Lorenzo Smerillo, Judith Swaddling, David Tripp. Special thanks go to Ellen Macnamara, to my editor Teresa Francis, and to Massimo Pallottino.

All mirrors, gems and alphabets are drawn by Sue Bird. Figs. 1, 2 and 3 are drawn by Sue Bird and Sue Goddard: Fig. 2 is adapted from Banti, 3, and Fig. 3 from L. Bonfante (ed.), *Etruscan Life and Afterlife*, Detroit 1986, map 5. Fig. 4: Pallottino, *Etruscans*, Fig. 9. Fig. 5: M. Pallottino, *Saggi di Antichità*, Rome 1979, 629–30. Fig. 6: *Thesaurus* 421. Fig. 7: drawn by Eva Wilson and reproduced by courtesy of B.T. Batsford Ltd. Fig. 8: E. Macnamara. Fig. 9: Paris, Bibliothèque Nationale. Fig. 10: A. Morandi, *MEFRA* 100 (1988), Fig. 3. Fig. 38: Morandi, *Epigrafia Italica*, 66. The numerals on p.22 are from *Thesaurus* 422.

University of California Press
Berkeley and Los Angeles

Designed by John Hawkins

Printed in Great Britain

Library of Congress Cataloging-in-Publication Data

Bonfante, Larissa.
Etruscan/Larissa Bonfante.
p. cm.—(Reading the past; v. 8)
Includes bibliographical references.
ISBN 0-520-07118-2 (alk. paper)
1. Etruscan language. 2. Inscriptions, Etruscan. 3. Inscriptions, Oscan-Umbrian. I. Title. II. Series.
P1078.B59 1990 90-31371
499'.94—dc20

Contents

1
Introduction

The Etruscans lived in central Italy, in an area bounded by the Arno and the Tiber rivers, from at least 700 BC (and probably earlier) to the first century BC. The Greeks knew them as Tyrrhenians, and gave this name to the sea which the Etruscans controlled to the west of the Italian peninsula, including some of the best harbours in the Mediterranean. The Romans called them Tusci or Etrusci. They evidently called themselves Rasna, or, according to Dionysius of Halicarnassus (first century BC), Rasenna.

New discoveries and new studies are allowing us to trace the lively commercial, cultural and political relations of the Etruscans and their contacts with the Greeks, Phoenicians, Latins and other inhabitants of Italy and Europe, from the beginning of their history as a people until the death of the Etruscan language. Like the ancient Greek cities or the Tuscan cities of the Renaissance, each Etruscan city had its own character, style and independence. There was never an Etruscan empire; there was, however, an Etruscan people who shared a language, religion, geographical location, customs and costumes which made them recognisably different from other peoples in Italy and the Mediterranean. They also shared a name; and, long before the Romans, they almost succeeded in uniting Italy.

The Etruscans brought 'civilisation', that is the culture of cities, including writing, to
1 the peoples of Italy and much of Europe, acting as the principal intermediaries between
the Greeks and the non-Greeks, or 'barbarians', of the west. Their political rule and
direct colonisation extended over much of the Italian peninsula; their commercial
2 activities and cultural influence reached much farther. The Etruscan cities were rivalled
only by those of Sicily and Southern Italy, founded by Greek settlers who brought culture to the west. The first of these Western Greeks, the Euboeans, settled in Pithekoussai (modern Ischia) in about 775 BC. The third great power in Italy, that of Carthage, was limited to western Sicily and Sardinia, but Phoenicians and Etruscans were commercially and politically allied and Phoenician influence was important for Etruscan art, religion and culture. It was Greek culture, however, which had the most visible impact on the Etruscans and, through them and the Romans, on Europe and the Mediterranean.

Etruscan history and civilisation and their influence are known to us from three types of evidence: Greek and Roman literary sources, archaeology and the Etruscan language – the subject of this book.

No Etruscan literature has come down to us, so the only ancient sources available are the writings of Greek and Roman authors. They describe the Etruscans as 'pirates', sea-going folk who traded and, when the occasion arose, raided rival ships and settlements. The maritime Etruscans in fact competed with Greek and Phoenician traders in the eighth and seventh centuries BC. During this international period, appropriately known as 'Orientalising' because of the influence from the east, the Greeks began their westward colonisation, attracted by Italy's rich mineral resources – iron and copper – which were controlled by the Etruscans.

1 Ancient Italy and its peoples, 8th–6th centuries BC.

When Greek historians turned their attention to this wealthy western people, they discussed the problem of their 'origins'. Herodotus (*c*.450 BC) quoted the Lydians, who claimed their ancestors had founded the Etruscan cities when they emigrated from Asia Minor, under the leadership of a certain Tyrrhenus. This theory was widely accepted in antiquity. In the first century BC Virgil could simply refer to the Etruscans as 'Lydians', and everyone understood him. Dionysius of Halicarnassus, a Greek historian writing at the time of Augustus, questioned this theory, though no one paid much attention in his own time. He argued that the Etruscans were in fact native to Italy. Not only did they call

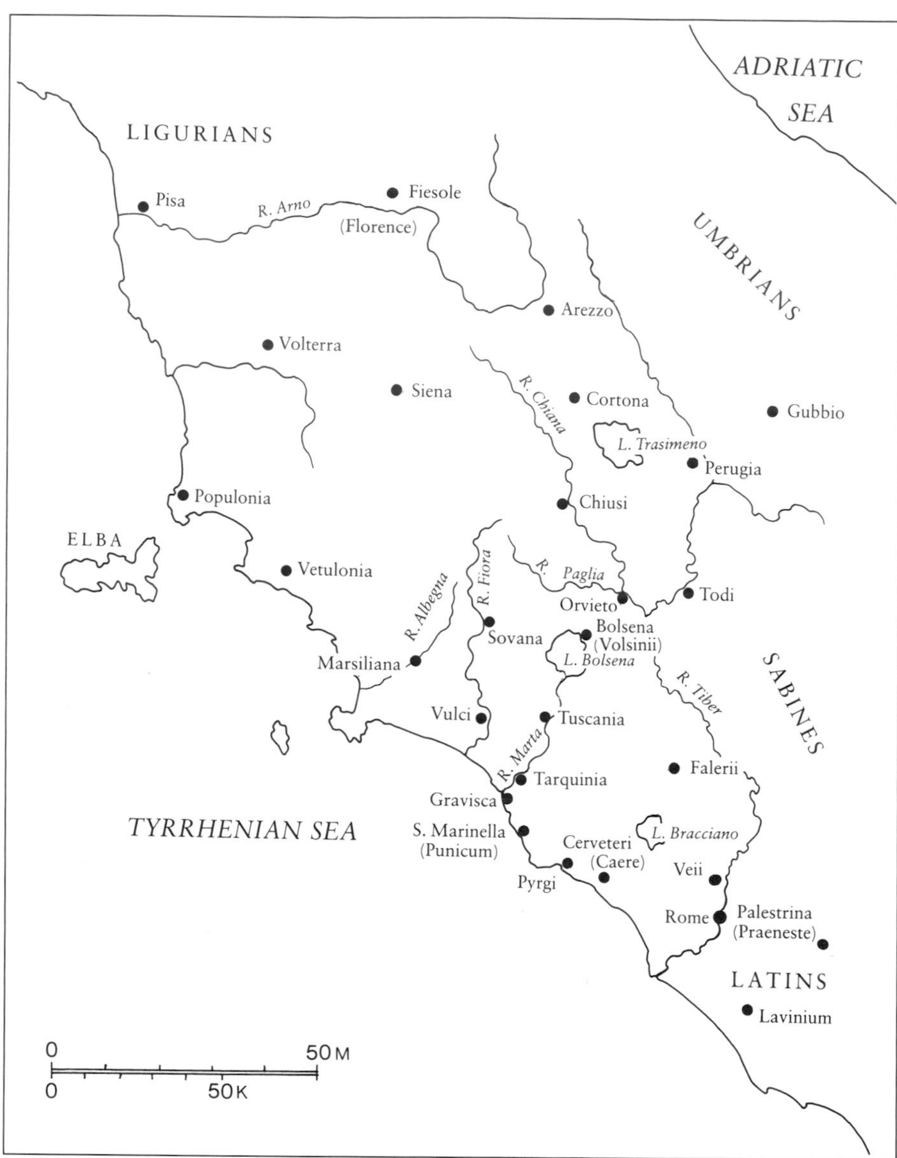

2 The Etruscan cities.

themselves Rasenna, and not Tyrrhenians, but, as he says, 'this most ancient nation does not resemble any other cities in their language or in their way of life, or customs' (1.30.2). Dionysius shrewdly related the problem of Etruscan origins to the nature of their language, and anticipated much of the modern discussion on the subject. The Lydian language is not at all close to Etruscan; nor has any archaeological evidence come forth, in the course of modern excavations of ancient Lydian cities, to confirm Herodotus' theory about an eastern origin. A third theory, wholly modern, suggesting that the Etruscans came down into Italy from the north, was based on nineteenth-century archaeological discoveries and theories, now known to be incorrect. The Etruscan presence in the Po Valley in fact resulted from conquest from the south.

3 The languages of ancient Italy.

Scholars today agree that, whatever the origins of the Etruscan people or the Etruscan language, the Etruscan civilisation as we know it developed on Italian soil. We must think in terms of a gradual transformation of groups in central Italy, in the prehistoric period from the end of the Bronze Age and throughout the Iron Age, into the historical people we know as the Etruscans, with their own special culture, social structure and economy.

Archaeological evidence is absolutely fundamental to our knowledge of Etruscan history. It allows us to situate the Etruscans in time and place and to recognise their foreign contacts, and provides reliable information about various phases of their art, culture and the extent of their influence. Furthermore, since we have no continuous narrative history, the dating system we use is based on the archaeological record.

The phases of Etruscan art do not correspond exactly to those of the art of their neighbours, the Greeks. For the sake of convenience, however, we use the same chronological terminology. The Iron Age period in the area of ancient Etruria (ninth to eighth centuries BC) is generally known as Villanovan (from the name of a site near Bologna where tombs from this phase have been excavated and dated). One does not, however, refer to the 'Villanovans', only to a 'Villanovan period'. The people of this period are now recognised by many scholars as 'proto-Etruscans'.

Writing does not appear in Etruria until about 700 BC, thus we have no direct evidence
3 as to the languages spoken in central Italy at this time. But archaeology shows that there was continuity between Villanovan centres and those of the Orientalising period (seventh century BC) and that it is very likely that the Etruscans were already living in this area and speaking the Etruscan language for some time before they began to write it down. They learned to write using the Greek alphabet adopted from their recently arrived neighbours at Pithekoussai and Cumae; and they began to record their language.

The Orientalising and Archaic (*c.* 600–400 BC) periods were the high point of Etruscan culture, art, power and influence. As the Roman historian Livy says, nearly all Italy, from the Alps to the straits of Sicily, rang to the fame of the Etruscan nation. The Po Valley, with its centre at Bologna (Felsina), was clearly Etruscanised by this time. Livy reports that twelve cities were founded there, to match the loose organisation of 'Twelve Peoples' in Etruria proper. In the south, Etruscan influence – and no doubt power – reached as far as Campania, to Capua and elsewhere. Rome's neighbour Praeneste (modern Palestrina) has yielded some of the most important tombs of the Orientalising period, the Barberini and Bernardini tombs, with Etruscan-style luxury articles and Etruscan inscriptions.

The most important city to show the effects of Etruscan 'civilising' was Rome itself. According to Roman tradition, Etruscan kings ruled in Rome from the end of the seventh century BC until 510/509 BC, when the Republic was established. Archaeology confirms the importance of Etruscan art and culture in Rome: temples were built in the Etruscan style and Etruscan inscriptions have been found. The name of one of the streets of ancient Rome, the Vicus Tuscus near the Capitoline Hill, long preserved the memory of their residence in the city. The Etruscans brought many innovations: writing, monumental architecture, the depiction of the human figure in art, luxurious customs, music, processions, chariots and games. But the Romans continued to speak Latin, beginning now to write it down using the Greek alphabet they learned from the Etruscans.

The fifth and fourth centuries saw a decline in Etruscan power. The loss of Rome as a base in the south and invasions of the Gauls from the north mark the end of its expansion. The coastal cities especially declined, although the cities of the interior – Volsinii (modern Orvieto), Chiusi, Volterra, Arezzo, Perugia and Fiesole – experienced a rise to prominence. In the final, Hellenistic, phase of Etruscan history (third century BC onwards) came the triumph of Roman prestige and power, the Romanisation of the oligarchic Etruscan noble families and the demise of the Etruscan language. Some of the longest inscriptions in Etruscan which survive from this period – sacred texts, mostly from the central Etruscan area around Lake Bolsena, rich in sanctuaries – constitute the latest recension of traditional texts originating from earlier periods. Whatever there may have been of Etruscan literature – drama, poetry, historical works – has perished. The Etruscans themselves stopped speaking their native language, became Romans, and abandoned, with their language, their tradition. There was thus no reason to preserve their texts by copying them in other books or volumes. A number of bilingual inscriptions, many of them epitaphs from the second and first centuries BC, testify to the change-over from Etruscan to Latin.

Although the Etruscans had ceased to exist as a separate people by the first century BC and certainly by the time of Augustus, Etruscan families and traditions survived in Rome. Maecenas, Augustus' friend and adviser, was a descendant of a noble Etruscan family. The emperor Claudius wrote a history of the Etruscans, in twenty volumes, which regrettably has not come down to us. His first wife, Urgulanilla, was Etruscan. In AD 408, when Alaric, king of the Goths, threatened to destroy Rome, some Etruscan priests went to the emperor, offering to perform certain magic rites and recite Etruscan prayers and incantations to ward off the enemy. But they were unsuccessful, for Rome was sacked, and it was the last time the Etruscan language was spoken.

The Etruscan language

The problem of Etruscan origins is encapsulated in the peculiarity of their language, which is different from any other in Italy or in Europe. Unlike all the other languages of Europe, except for Basque, Hungarian and Finnish, Etruscan does not belong to the great Indo-European family of languages spoken from around 4000 BC by groups of people migrating from a region in central Europe around the Baltic area, as far east as India and as far west as Ireland. The only known related language is that preserved in a remarkable inscription, written in an alphabet and language akin to Etruscan on a stele
4 with the figure of a warrior, found in 1885 at Kaminia on the northern Aegean island of Lemnos and dated to the late sixth century BC. It has 98 letters, forming 33 words. In 1928 Italian archaeologists in Lemnos found similar fragmentary inscriptions on sherds of locally made pottery. These were of vital importance, for they showed that the language was actually spoken in Lemnos: the stele had not been imported from elsewhere in the Mediterranean. We know, therefore, that a dialect close to Etruscan was spoken at Lemnos before the Athenian conquest of the island in the second half of the sixth century BC. This dialect was different from all

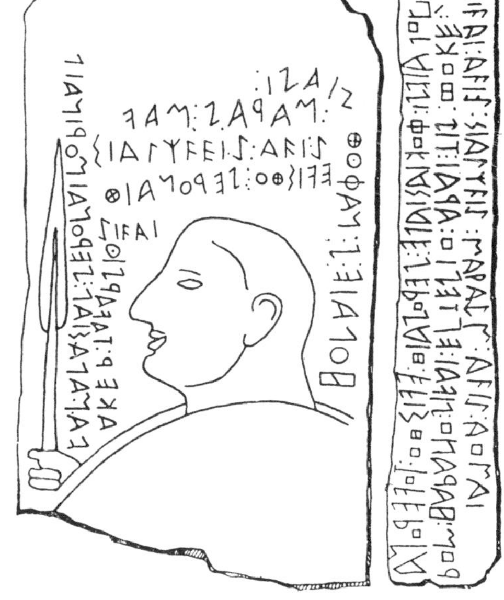

4 Stone stele from Lemnos, 6th century BC. Athens, National Museum.

other languages spoken in the area. We do not know, however, how and when it came to be spoken there.

The Etruscan language which we read on the earliest inscriptions in Etruria had evidently already been spoken in the area for a long time, and it provides proof of the Etruscans' relationship with their neighbours. For instance, the commercial and cultural contacts they had with the Greeks are reflected in their vocabulary: Greek names for drinking vessels were taken into the language (e.g. *culichna,* from *kylix,* 'cup'). A very large number of Greek mythological figures are depicted and named in Etruscan art and inscriptions. We find Etruscan words in Umbrian, and most of the so-called Iguvine Tablets from Gubbio, in the Umbrian dialect, are written in the Etruscan alphabet. We also find, on the other hand, Umbrian and Latin words in Etruscan. For example, Etruscan *neftś* is certainly of Latin origin: it comes from Latin *nepos,* 'nephew'. The Latin word was adopted by the Etruscans, just as the word *cousin* was adopted from French into English. *Vinum*, 'wine', also comes from Latin. Conversely, Etruscan influence in Rome left clear traces in the Latin language. A close study of Latin vocabulary reveals many words which were originally Etruscan, most of them connected with luxurious living and higher culture, including writing. Four words dealing with writing came into Latin by way of the Etruscan language, confirming the Etruscan transmission of the Greek alphabet to the Romans: *elementum,* whose earlier meaning was 'letter of the alphabet', *litterae,* 'writing' (originally derived from Greek *diphthera,* 'skin', a material on which people wrote); *stilus,* 'writing implement', and *cera,* 'wax' (for wax tablets on which to take notes).

The main problems confronting scholars studying the Etruscan language are, first, that it resembles no other language in Europe or elsewhere: in direct contrast with Linear B, which turned out to be an unknown script used for a known language, Etruscan is an unknown language written in a known script – the alphabet. Secondly, no literature survives: we have no narrative texts, no history, poetry or drama. Thirdly, the 13,000 Etruscan inscriptions that have come down to us are mostly short: dedications or epitaphs, with names, human and divine, titles, and a few common nouns, numbers and verbs. The few longer ones are technical: religious texts, prayers, rites and contracts. Attempting to solve these difficulties, scholars have studied the Etruscan language in a variety of ways, using bilingual inscriptions and glosses as well as linguistic and cultural-archaeological methods.

5 Bilingual texts include three gold tablets written in Phoenician and Etruscan, found in 1964 at Pyrgi, the port of Caere, as well as some thirty Etruscan-Latin inscriptions. There are also numerous 'picture bilinguals', in which labels or captions identify pictures on wall-paintings, gems and engraved mirrors. Particularly promising is the comparison of Etruscan religious inscriptions with those of their neighbours. The Iguvine Tablets, for example, in the Umbrian language, are 'quasi-bilinguals', written partly in the Etruscan and partly in a Latin alphabet, and resemble religious inscriptions of Etruria in both structure and content.

Glosses comprise the only non-archaeological epigraphical evidence available to us concerning the Etruscan language. They are definitions or marginal notes, intended by ancient authors to explain Etruscan words which appeared in Greek or Latin texts, including many words which referred to the *etrusca disciplina,* the religious sphere of divination which the Romans imported from their neighbours. They refer to birds, plants

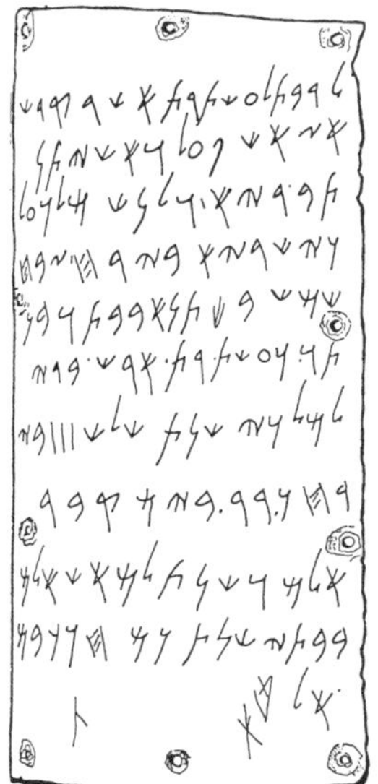

5 Gold tablets from Pyrgi, *c.* 500 BC. Inscribed in Etruscan (centre and right) and Phoenician (left) (*TLE* 874, *CIE* 6314).

and rituals: for example *capys,* 'eagle'. Other glosses explain *atrium,* the 'entrance' of the typical Roman house; *ais,* 'god'; *lucumo,* 'king', and *clan,* 'son'.

Important contributions have also been made by the study of names and syntax and of the transformation of Greek words brought into Etruscan, such as the names of Greek gods and heroes inscribed on Etruscan gems and mirrors. Etruscan pronunciation, and the changes it underwent during the approximately seven centuries when Etruscan was spoken and written, can be reconstructed because these changes were regularly reflected in the spelling, which remained, it seems, strictly phonetic. The Etruscans never developed an 'historical' spelling as in English, where for example the *oo* of 'spoon', once pronounced with a long *o,* as in 'whole', now has the same sound as *u* in 'rule'.

Etruscan cannot be interpreted through any kind of 'etymological' method which claims connections, for example, with Albanian and Basque, Hebrew, Turkish, etc. Such connections are based on accidental, superficial resemblances with other languages or language families, not on any real relationship. As a language, Etruscan is in fact isolated. For this reason, the most fruitful method has been the cultural-archaeological approach, in which an inscription is considered in its historical context and in close relation to the monument or object on which it appears. A good example of inscriptions studied in such a manner is the Etruscan book reconstructed from linen bands later used to wrap a mummy, now in Zagreb (see p. 27). These were originally part of a ritual book, a liturgical calendar listing names of gods, dates, and types of offerings to be made.

The discovery of the Pyrgi tablets, hailed as the long-sought-after 'bilingual' in 1964, marked a turning-point in Etruscan studies. It coincided with, and was in part responsible for, a new focus in the study of the Etruscan language, which can be summarised as follows:

1. A view of the historical and geographical context of the inscriptions as having been made in Italy at a specific time is in keeping with the growing consciousness of the Etruscans as deeply involved in ancient Italy as well as in the ancient Mediterranean.
2. A new study of monuments which have been in museums and collections for a

hundred years or more has resulted in discoveries as important as those from newly excavated material, restoring archaeological and historical contexts of objects uprooted from their original environment by 'treasure hunting' excavations.

3. Collections of all known inscriptions have been made or are in progress. Such *Corpora,* begun in the nineteenth century, have been started up again and new ones inaugurated in a remarkable wave of international collaboration: these include the *Corpus of Etruscan Inscriptions (CIE)*; the *Thesaurus*, listing all Etruscan words to be found in inscriptions and glosses; and the *Corpus of Etruscan Mirrors (CSE)*, containing many interesting names of mythological figures. The guiding spirit behind all these projects has been Massimo Pallottino, who was also responsible for the *Testimonia Linguae Etruscae (TLE)* a selection of the most important inscriptions, listed according to their provenance. The appearance of a fully-fledged grammar of Etruscan (Pfiffig 1975) – though criticised by some scholars as over optimistic – has helped to stimulate further study.

Note on the transcription of Etruscan letters

(all these are rough equivalents)

𐌙 = *ch* (*kh*), aspirate: as in English *kin*.

⊙ O = *th*, aspirate: as in English *ten*.

Φ = *ph*, aspirate: as in English *pan*.

𐌔 ⊞ X = *s*, sibilant: as in English *sin*.

M = *ś*, sibilant: perhaps pronounced as in English *shin*.

Note. Aspirate consonants, for which there are no signs in English, were pronounced with an audible breath puff, or 'h' sound, following a *k*, *p* or *t* sound. Initial *k*, *p* and *t* have a somewhat similar sound in English. In Etruscan, as in Greek, Φ was pronounced with such a plosive sound, not like an *f*; that is why a new letter had to be found for the sound of *f*, which the Greeks did not have.

Etruscan had voiceless consonants or stops, *k* (and *c* and *q*), *p* and *t;* but not the voiced (sonant) consonants *g*, *b* and *d* (these are so called because their pronunciation involves the use of the vocal cords).

Etruscan sounds are here transcribed in lower-case italics, and letters in italic capitals.

2
The Etruscan Language

The Alphabet

Since a historical people is usually defined by its language, strictly speaking we can only identify these inhabitants of central Italy as 'Etruscans' from the moment when we first begin to see texts written in the Etruscan language, around 700 BC. These were written in the same script we use today, the alphabet, in which each sign originally represented a different sound. From the alphabetic script of the Phoenicians, without vowels, was derived the Greek alphabet, in which certain consonantal sounds were adapted to signify vowels: A, E (H = long *e*), I, O (Ω = *omega*, 'large o' or long *o*) and Y. An impressive sign of historical conservation is the fact that schoolchildren today still recite the alphabet in roughly the same order in which the Greeks first received it, almost 3,000 years ago.

As a prestigious sign of the new Orientalising style and as a status symbol, the alphabet decorates a number of Etruscan objects placed in rich tombs of the seventh century BC. These 'model' alphabets, taken directly from the Greek alphabet as brought west by the Euboeans, bear witness to the speed with which this new development was adopted. The Etruscans considered the letters of the alphabet decorative, perhaps even magical, and copied them on various objects. They wrote from right to left, like the Phoenicians and other ancient Semitic peoples.

Writing implements decorated with these letters were placed in the tombs of wealthy, important people. Examples include an ivory writing tablet from Marsiliana d'Albegna (Archaeological Museum, Florence), originally decorated with gold leaf, meant to be worn as a pendant; a bucchero (shiny black pottery) container in the shape of a rooster, with a crested lid, which may once have held a coloured liquid like ink (Metropolitan Museum, New York); and a tall, slender bucchero vase, a brush or pen holder, from the Regolini-Galassi tomb in Cerveteri, now in the Vatican Museum, covered not only with the letters of the alphabet but with syllables as well.

The alphabet of twenty-six signs displayed on all these objects is called a 'model'
alphabet. Some of its letters – 𐌁, 𐌂, 𐌃, O – are never used in Etruscan inscriptions 6
(so, too, Italian children learn the signs *k*, *j*, *w* and *y*, which never appear in Italian words). Etruscan has no *b*, *d*, or *g* (voiced stops), and no *o*, but these signs are included in the alphabet, which faithfully reproduces the Greek model from which the Etruscan derived. Of the four signs for *s*, only two were regularly used at any one time or place.

There are, to date, seventy-five known Etruscan inscriptions from the seventh century BC, a very respectable quantity when compared with Greek inscriptions from this period. These and later examples show the steps in the adaptation of the alphabet to the Etruscan language. The sound *u* (written V or Y) was regularly substituted for *o*. The Greek Φ, an aspirate, was pronounced as a *p* followed by the sound of 'h': it was not an *f* sound, as it is today. A new sign, 8, represented the sound *f*, unknown in Greek. In fact we owe the sound *f* to the Etruscans, who passed it on to the Latins, Oscans, Umbrians and

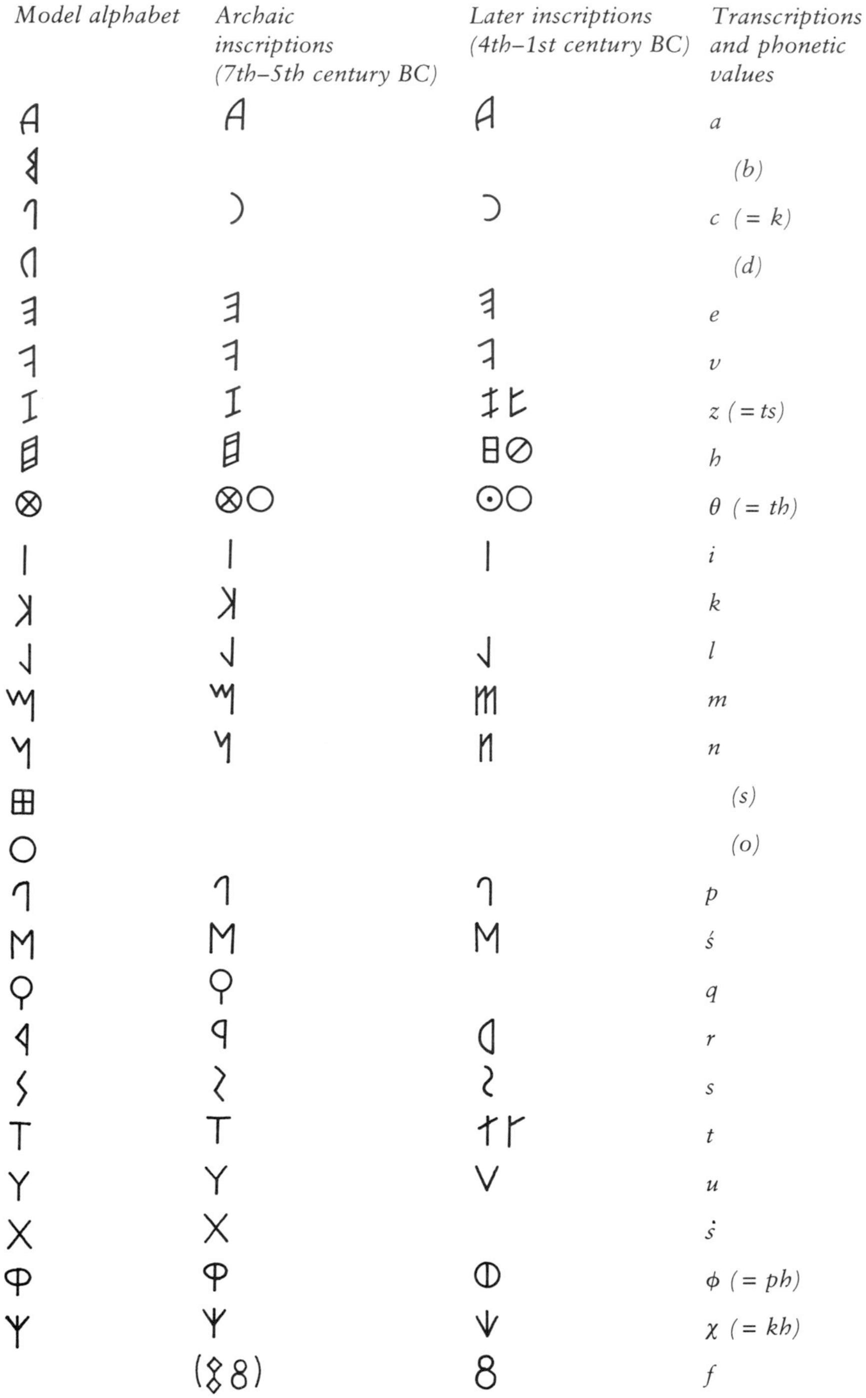

Model alphabet	*Archaic inscriptions (7th–5th century BC)*	*Later inscriptions (4th–1st century BC)*	*Transcriptions and phonetic values*
𐌀	𐌀	𐌀	*a*
𐌁			*(b)*
𐌂	𐌂	𐌂	*c (= k)*
𐌃			*(d)*
𐌄	𐌄	𐌄	*e*
𐌅	𐌅	𐌅	*v*
𐌆	𐌆	𐌆 𐌆	*z (= ts)*
𐌇	𐌇	𐌇 ⊘	*h*
𐌈	𐌈 ○	⊙ ○	*θ (= th)*
𐌉	𐌉	𐌉	*i*
𐌊	𐌊		*k*
𐌋	𐌋	𐌋	*l*
𐌌	𐌌	𐌌	*m*
𐌍	𐌍	𐌍	*n*
𐌎			*(s)*
𐌏			*(o)*
𐌐	𐌐	𐌐	*p*
𐌑	𐌑	𐌑	*ś*
𐌒	𐌒		*q*
𐌓	𐌓	𐌓	*r*
𐌔	𐌔	𐌔	*s*
𐌕	𐌕	𐌕 𐌕	*t*
𐌖	𐌖	V	*u*
𐌗	𐌗		*ṡ*
𐌘	𐌘	𐌘	*φ (= ph)*
𐌙	𐌙	𐌙	*χ (= kh)*
	(𐌚 8)	8	*f*

6 Etruscan alphabets.

Veneti in Italy, and beyond to Northern Europe. In reading Etruscan transcriptions of Greek names, it is important to remember that the Etruscans changed the voiced stops *g*, *b* and *d* to *k*, *p* and *t* (voiceless) whenever these appeared in foreign words – Greek, Latin or Umbrian. Thus from the Greek word *thriambos* came the Latin word *triumpus* or *triumphus*, 'victory celebration', by way of Etruscan.

All alphabets, when first used, are strictly phonetic, and Etruscan spelling remained so. The alphabetic system changed twice, first when the Greek model alphabet was adapted to the needs of the Etruscan language, then some time around 400 BC various other changes culminated in the creation of the so-called 'neo-Etruscan' alphabet. Several letters disappeared. *K* continued to be used in the northern cities, as did the sibilant M (*ś*). An inscription can accordingly be dated, not absolutely, but in general terms, as belonging to the Archaic period or to the later period (fourth to first centuries BC).

The loss of vowels in Etruscan spelling after the first syllable, resulting in clusters of consonants, was due to an intensive stress accent which around 500 BC affected Etruscan as well as other languages of Italy (Latin, Umbrian, Oscan, Sabellian). The first syllable was heavily accented, with the result that following vowels weakened (*a* > *e* > *i*), and eventually dropped out. This abbreviation, or syncope, is most obvious in the later, neo-Etruscan inscriptions of the fourth century BC and the Hellenistic period. On Etruscan mirrors, for example, we find the Greek name Alexandros written in the abbreviated form Alcsentre, and even Elcsntre. Ramutha (a woman's name) becomes Ramtha; Rasenna (the name of the Etruscans) Rasna; Klytaimestra (Clytemnestra) becomes Clutumsta, then Clutmsta; *turice,* 'gave', becomes *turce*. (The pronunciation of English also provides example of this: both 'Leicester' and 'Worcester' are pronounced in a 'syncopated' way.) This loss of vowels was only partly compensated for by nasal liquids (the 'l' in Atlnta, for the Greek name of the female athlete Atalanta, was pronounced something like the final syllable of English 'castle'). Conversely, sometimes in the internal syllables extra vowels were inserted in consonant clusters to make words easier to pronounce. This tendency accounts for the transformation of the Greek name of the goddess Artemis into Aritimi, of the Etruscan name for Herakles (Hercle) into Herecele and of Menrva (Minerva) into Menerva.

As stated above, the direction of Etruscan writing normally goes from right to left, the reverse of classical Greek, Latin or English. In the Archaic period inscriptions are occasionally written *boustrophedon*, 'as the ox ploughs' – one line going from left to right, the next from right to left, and so on. This was the system used by the early Greeks, before they settled on writing left to right (*c.*550 BC). Examples of Etruscan writing from left to right do occur on some mirrors, where they are clearly dictated by a desire for symmetry or to keep the label close to the figure. Inscriptions of the third century BC or later, under Latin influence, also read from left to right. In this late period some inscriptions in the Etruscan language were written in the Latin alphabet; and some, in the Latin language, with Etruscan letters.

In the earliest inscriptions the words are not separated at all, the letters running on one after the other (*scriptio continua*). From the sixth century BC, words are often divided from each other by one, two or more dots placed vertically above each other. Sometimes this 'punctuation' separates groups of letters or syllables within a word: such syllabic punctuation constitutes a peculiar feature of Etruscan writing in certain periods.

Pronunciation

Consonants

Since they could not pronounce the voiced stop *g*, the Etruscans used the third letter of the Greek alphabet, *gamma* Γ, 𐌂 or (, with the value of *k*. Thus for the sound *k* (English *think*) they used three signs: *K* (𐌊) before *a (ka); C* (𐌂) before *e* and *i (ce, ci)* ; and *Q* (𐌒) before *u (qu)*. The same system was used by the early Latins, who imitated the Etruscan. The K of early Latin survived before *a* in a few words, such as *Kalendae,* from which 'calendar' derives. (In English the same three letters survive with the sound of *k: ke, ca, qu.*)

The influence of Etruscan on the Latin alphabet is shown by the fact that the Latins followed the Etruscan use of the Greek *gamma,* written as a C, to represent the sound of *k (cena, cura, catena, civis, corium)*. Originally in Latin the letter C could be pronounced as *k* (*Caesar*, from which comes the German word *Kaiser*) and also as *g* (*Caius,* pronounced *Gaius*). It was not until about 250 BC that the Romans introduced a new letter, G (which was merely a slightly changed C), specifically for the voiced stop *g*. In order to avoid changing the order of the alphabet, this new letter G took the place of the Greek letter Z, which the Latins had inherited but did not use; the 'slot' was therefore available. Later, in the first century BC, when more intimate contact with the Greeks made it necessary to write Greek words, the Latins reinstated the letter Z, which, having lost its place, was put at the end – where it still is today.

In general, pronunciation was harsh. We have seen that the voiced stops *b, d, g* were substituted by *p, t, k*. The aspirated sounds (*ph, th, ch, ts*) also gave a rough texture to speech. The letter Z (𐌆) in Etruscan had a voiceless sound, as for example in English *gets, eats,* and not as in *zeal.* Some scholars have suggested that the modern *gorgia toscana* so obvious in Florence and Siena today (Coca Cola = 'hola hola') derives from Etruscan.

The Etruscans had a sound *f* (pronounced more or less as in English *find, stuff*). The Greeks did not have this sound, nor did they have a sign for it. At first the Etruscans approximated the sound with the two sounds *w* and *h*, written as 𐌅𐌇. Later they adopted a new sign, 𐌚 (its origin is obscure). The Latins, however, kept the first element of *vh,* 𐌅: F, the letter familiar to us with the sound of *f*.

The Etruscan 𐌅 (*digamma*, here transcribed as *v*) was bilabial, like English *w* or Latin *v* in *vincit.* Diphthongs like *au* are frequently spelled *av: lautni > lavtni; aule > avle.*

Vowels

The Etruscan vowel system is simple. There are only four vowels: *a, e, i, u*. In Etruscan the letter *A* is always pronounced *ah,* as in *father; I* is always *ee,* as in *machine; U* is *oo,* as in *rule* or *moon. U* always substitutes for *o,* which does not exist, as we have seen. *E* is *eh,* as in *elf:* it was a very closed vowel, almost like *i,* with which it was in fact often interchanged. So we see both *ica* and *eca, mini* and *mine, cliniiaras* and *clenar,* etc. The Greek name Iason (Jason) becomes Easun; and the Etruscan genitive form *-ial* often becomes *-eal.* Etruscan had only short vowels, like several modern languages, for example Spanish and Romanian. There were no long vowels like Greek *eta* (H) or *omega* (Ω). Since the letter *H* or 𐌇 was not needed to represent a long *e*, as in Greek, it was therefore available to represent the sound of *h,* as in English *hat* today. It already had the value of *h* in some Greek dialects.

Greek diphthongs are usually preserved, except of course that *oi* becomes *ui*. In later inscriptions (fifth to first centuries BC), *ai* often becomes *ei* or even *e*: thus the Greek name Aias (Ajax) is written as Aivas, Eivas or Evas in Etruscan. *Graikos,* 'Greek', written *Graecus* in Latin, becomes *creice* in Etruscan. There is a general trend toward the simplification of two different vowels, forming a diphthong, into a simple vowel. *Eu* sometimes becomes *u* in Etruscan: for example, the name of Castor's brother Pollux, Polydeukes in Greek, in Etruscan becomes Pultuce.

Grammar

Etruscan is an inflected language. There are different endings, or inflections, for nouns, pronouns and verbs. Though the limited amount of materials at our disposal precludes the systematic setting out of an Etruscan 'grammar', and even the use of conventional grammatical terms is anything but certain, there are certain forms we can recognise.

Note: For Etruscan personal names and other words cited in the text, see the Appendices.

Nouns
Here is an example of a declension:

	Singular	Plural
Nominative and Accusative	*clan*, 'son'	*clenar*, 'the sons'
Genitive, 'of'	*clens*, 'of the son'	*clenaraśi* } 'to the sons'
Dative, 'to'	*clensi*, 'to the son'	*cliniiaras* } 'to the sons'
Locative, 'in'	**clenthi*, 'in the son'	

(* this form is not attested, only hypothetical)

Common nouns have no special endings for masculine, feminine or neuter.

Only personal names have gender in Etruscan. Many masculine names end in *e* (Greek and Latin equivalents are given where known):

Hercle (Gk Herakles; Lat. Hercules), Menle (Gk Menelaos), Achle (Gk Achilles), Zimite (Gk Diomedes), Tite Cale (Lat. Titus Calus), Aule (Lat. Aulus), Taitle (Gk Daidalos; Lat. Daedalus), Sime, Artile.

Others end in a consonant:

Evas (Gk Aias; Lat. Ajax), Arnth (Lat. Arruns), Larth (Lat. Lars), Velthur, Laran.

Feminine names end in *-i* or *-a:*

Uni (Lat. Juno), Menrva (Lat. Minerva), Clutmsta (Gk Klytemnestra, Klytaimestra), Ati, Seianti, Lasa

and sometimes in *-u:*

Zipu, Thanchvilu.

Names of gods often have the nominative in *-s:*
Fufluns (no precise equivalent; Gk Dionysos; Lat. Bacchus), Sethlans (no precise equivalent; Gk Hephaistos), Tins (no precise equivalent; Gk Zeus), Selvans (Lat. Silvanus).

Otherwise male and female gods' names may have the same endings, whether consonant:
Turan (no precise equivalent; Gk Aphrodite), Thanr (f), Malavisch (f), Laran (m)

or vowel:
Pacha (Lat. Bacchus), Aplu (Gk Apollo).

The genitive is formed by adding *-s* or *-l* to the stem, often inserting a vowel between the stem and the ending. After a liquid consonant (*l, r*), *-us* is used:
Velthur > Velthurus, Vel > Velus, Thanchvil > Tanchvilus.

The genitive ending in *-al* is added to feminine names ending in *-i:*
Uni > Unial, Ati > Atial

and to masculine names ending in *-s:*
Laris > Larisal

or ending in a dental:
Arnth > Arnthal.

Sometimes a special ending in *-sa* or *-isa* designates the patronymic, 'son of'.
aule velimna larthal clan = *aule velimna larthalisa,* 'Aules Velimna, son of Larth'.

Thus the genitive expresses possession (*arnthal clan,* 'son of Arnth'). It also expresses dedication (as does the dative in Latin):
ecn turce . . . selvansl, 'this [she] gave to Selvans'.

There is also a dative form in *-si:*
mi titasi cver menache, 'I was offered to Tita as a gift'.

The plural is formed by adding *-r (-ar, -er, -ur).* An uncommon shift of the stem vowel in the plural occurs in *clan* > *clenar*, 'son' > 'sons'.

The locative ending is *-thi.*

Pronouns

1. Personal pronouns
   First person: Nom. *mi,* 'I'
   Acc. *mini*, 'me'
   No other case forms are known.

   Third person: (animate, male and female) *an,* 'he', 'she'
   (inanimate, neuter) *in*, 'it'
   No other case forms are known.

2. Demonstrative pronouns
   Nom. *ita, eta, ta,* 'this'; or *ika, eca, ca,* 'this'
   Acc. *etan, tn,* 'this'; or *can, cn, ecn,* 'this'
   Loc. *calti,* 'in this'; or *eclthi, clthi,* 'in this'

Adjectives

A variety of forms denote adjectives:

1. Of quality
   aisiu, 'divine' (from *ais*, 'god')
   hinthiu, 'infernal' (from *hintha*, 'underworld')

2. Possession or reference
   aisna, eisna, 'pertaining to god', 'divine'
   pachana 'of or pertaining to Bacchus' (from Pacha, 'Bacchus')
   śuthina, 'of or pertaining to the tomb' (from *śuthi,* 'tomb').

   Family names in *-na* belong to this type. But in southern Etruscan cities the family name (equivalent to our last name) ends in *-s: aule vipiiennas.* This may derive from a genitive form (*-s*), 'of the Vipiienna', etc., a formation similar to della Robbia, di Giovanni, etc. in Italian, and names with *de* in French, *von* in German and *van* in Dutch. (In fact, when an inscription gives a name in the genitive we often cannot tell whether the nominative ends in *s* or not: Atnas, Pulenas, Vipinanas, etc.)

3. Collective
   math, mathcva, 'full of drink' (from *math* 'honeyed wine')
   srencva, 'full of ornament' (from *sren,* 'picture' or 'figure')
   flerchva, 'group of sacred statues, offerings' (from *fler,* 'offering, sacrifice').

Adverbs and Conjunctions

The conjunction *-c* is equivalent to Latin *-que,* meaning 'and'. *Um,* enclitic *-m,* also means 'and'.

Alpan or *alpnu* is an adverb, 'gladly', 'willingly'; it can also mean 'as a gift', 'offering'.

Verbs

The present active form consists of the root, *ar, zich, tur.* Another form ends in *-a*:
ara, tva, as in *eca sren tva,* 'this picture shows'.

The best-known form is the third person singular past (aorist). In the active form the ending is *-ce*:
turce, 'he/she gave'
svalce, 'he/she lived'
lupuce, 'he/she died'
muluvanice, 'he/she made/built'.

This can be distinguished from the passive form, *-che,* for the first person singular:
mi . . . zichuche, 'I was written'
mi titasi cver menache, 'I was offered to Tita as a gift'.

The text of the Zagreb mummy (see p. 27 below) gives examples of imperatives. One type of imperative consists of the simple verbal root (as in the Indo-European languages):
vacl ar, 'make (*ar*) the libation (*vacl*).

Another imperative, ending in *-ti, -th* or *-thi*, is used for the second person singular:
racth tura, 'prepare the incense'.

Another form seems to be a passive participle of obligation, ending in *-ri* or *-eri*:

huthiś zathrumiś flerchva nathunsl . . . thezeri-c, 'and on the 26th the sacrifices for Neptune are to be made'.

Numerals

Etruscan numerals are known from funerary inscriptions recording the age of the deceased and from the 'Tuscania dice', on which the first six numbers are written out in words rather than shown by dots, as usual. We therefore know the first six numbers:

thu, zal, ci, śa, mach, huth

Their order was recognised because in antiquity the sum of each of the two opposite sides of the die added up to seven: *mach* + *zal* = seven; *thu* + *huth* = seven; *ci* + *śa* = seven. Other clues led to the identification of each particular number, so that the order given above is generally accepted today.

What these numerals show, beyond any shadow of a doubt, is the non-Indo-European nature of the Etruscan language. Basic words like numbers and names of relationships are often similar in the Indo-European languages, for they derive from the same root.

Another peculiarity of Etruscan is the formation of numbers by subtraction, a system found also in Latin. Given the cultural influence of the Etruscans in Rome, Latin may have derived it from Etruscan. In Etruscan, 17 = 20 − 3, 18 = 20 − 2, 19 = 20 − 1. In Latin we have *duodeviginti, undeviginti*. Multiples of 10 are formed with the addition of *-alc* or *-alch*. (An asterisk indicates forms not attested in inscriptions.)

1	*thu*	10	*śar*	30	*ci-alch* (*ce-alch*)
2	*zal, es(a)l*	16	*huth-zar*	40	*śe-alch*
3	*ci*	17	*ci-em zathrum*	50	*muv-alch* (**mach-alch*)
4	*śa*	18	*esl-em zathrum*	60	**huth-alch*
5	*mach*	19	*thun-em zathrum*	70	*semph-alch*(?)
6	*huth*	20	*zathrum*	80	*cezp-alch*(?)
7	*semph*(?)	27	*ci-em-ce-alch*	90	**nurph-alch*(?)
8	*cezp*(?)	28	*esl-em-ce-alch*	100	?
9	*nurph*(?)	29	*thun-em-ce-alch*	1000	?

Etruscan	*Roman*	*Arabic*
I	I	1
Λ	V	5
X	X	10
↑	L	50
C ⁎	C	100
⊙	C or M?	100 or 1000?
⊕	M or M̄?	1000 or 10,000?

Etruscan numerals

3
Writing Materials and Methods

Books and writing were very important to the Etruscans throughout their history: Pallottino has even called them the 'People of the Book'. They wrote on a variety of materials: bronze, clay, plaster, stone, gold, lead, cloth, wax, and perhaps papyrus. We know from Roman historians that books made of linen, *libri lintei,* were used in Rome, and Etruscan ritual texts were also written on linen. It was imported from Egypt by the seventh century BC and was also woven in Etruria. In Etruscan art such books are usually shown as attributes of priests or *haruspices* (diviners), and are sometimes folded, not rolled up like scrolls. For example, a folded linen book appears on the lid of a funerary urn from Chiusi, on the bed or couch of the deceased, under the characteristic pointed hat of the Etruscan *haruspex*. Perhaps a similar book is represented by the folded cloth at the bedside of the owners of the Tomb of the Reliefs in Cerveteri, where the furnishings of a normal upper-class household – including plates, ropes, a gaming-board, dishes and pets – were all shown in brightly painted relief on the walls of their house-like tomb.

The most famous linen book, and the only one to have come down to us in anything like its original form, is the cloth recycled as wrappings for an Egyptian mummy, now in Zagreb (see also p. 27). This book was a liturgical calendar, and the cloth – of which almost 3.5 m in length and 35 cm in width is preserved – was compact and tightly woven, clearly meant to be written on. The surface may have been treated in a special way so that the ink, which was probably applied with a brush, would not be absorbed. Two types of ink were used: black ('ivory black') for the text, and red (cinnabar, 100 per cent HgS) for the vertical lines dividing the columns. Red was also used to underline special sections in the text, evidently to help the officiating priest find his place in the ritual by unfolding the book gradually and turning to the appropriate section. The right-hand end of the cloth is much more worn than the left: this was perhaps the beginning of the book (it would of course have been at the back, as in Hebrew books).

Scrolls are represented on several monuments. We cannot be certain what material was actually used; perhaps papyrus imported from Egypt, or possibly linen, like the folded books.

Wax tablets were used for memos, letters, tallies and other records. Bronze styli used to
7 incise the letters in the wax have been preserved, many of them decorated with attractive bronze figurines. The frames of these wax tablets were usually made of wood, though some especially precious ones might have been made from ivory or bone. They were in two parts hinged together as a diptych, so they could be closed and the message, inscribed on the wax surface with a stylus, protected from wear as well as prying eyes. The date of the Marsiliana ivory tablet with a 'model' alphabet, mid-seventh century BC, puts it in the period when the alphabet was still a novelty, in Greece as well as in Etruria. On a relief
8 from Chiusi, a man is shown recording something, probably the prizes won in a competition. The date of this relief, about 500 BC, is contemporary with a story recorded by the historian Livy (2.12): Caius Mucius Scaevola's attempt to kill the Etruscan king – or

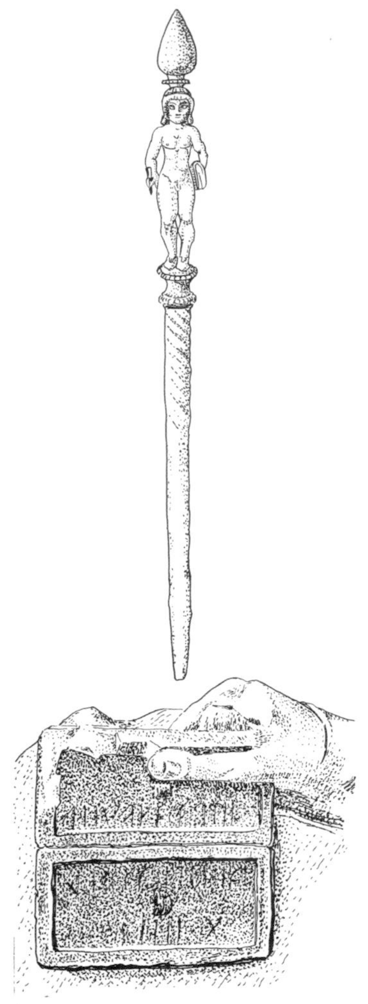

8 Detail of a stone relief from Chiusi, *c.* 500 BC: a secretary recording prizes on a hinged tablet. Palermo Archaeological Museum.

7 *Left* Writing implements: bronze stylus, and relief showing wax tablets.

'tyrant' – Porsenna, who was besieging Rome. Porsenna's secretary, who was seated writing next to the king, was dressed so elegantly that Scaevola mistook him for Porsenna: evidently the secretary played an important role in Etruscan society. Yet there was nothing like a 'scribal' caste or group. The awkwardness of many inscriptions, such as those denoting ownership, shows that literacy was widespread – at least as much as in other ancient societies in the same historical period.

A large number of inscriptions in Etruria have been preserved on terracotta. On a tile from Capua (see p. 27) an inscription was incised in the clay while it was still wet: this is the easiest way of writing on clay. A seventh-century vase in Villa Giulia in Rome has the letters 'embossed' in relief, in a decorative pattern below the neck. The sarcophagus of Seianti Hanunia Tlesnasa has its handsome letters cut into the clay. Terracotta urns of the later period have the inscription either incised or painted on. On vases, 'labels' identifying the figures depicted were often painted on the clay, before or after firing. In the Archaic period the following Etruscan inscription was scratched on the foot of a handsome imported Greek vase, an Attic cup by the painter Oltos (*c.*500 BC):

itun turuce venel atelinas tinas cliniiaras

'This gave (*turuce*) Venel Atelinas to Tina's sons', or 'Venel Atelinas gave this to the sons of Zeus' (i.e. the Dioskouroi).

The Etruscan owner of a Greek vase often wrote a dedication to a god in this way.

Bronze was a material widely used in Italy for inscriptions. The Umbrian Iguvine tablets, the Oscan Agnone plaque (see Chapter 6) and the *Monumentum Ancyranum*, a Greek translation of Augustus' testament, are outstanding examples of this type of document. (For the Etruscans, terracotta and bronze were not secondary materials; they were what they worked best, in contrast to the Greeks and Romans, who normally recorded their *acta publica,* their public decisions and deeds, on stone). The letters of the text inscribed on a bronze model of a sheep's liver from Piacenza (see p. 29) were incised after casting, when the surface was already rigid; if they had been traced on the clay model, one would expect them to be rounded.

The largest number of Etruscan inscriptions on bronze occur on 1,000 or so figured mirrors (about 3,000 mirrors have survived in all). With a few notable exceptions whose
decoration is in relief, the decoration on the reverse of these is engraved. A smaller but 11–21
important category of bronze objects with inscriptions encompasses votive statues and 38–9
statuettes. These include the beautiful large Chimaera of Arezzo. On the beast's paw is the inscription *tinścvil,* cut into the wax model before the bronze was cast, declaring it to be a 'gift to Tinia', that is Zeus or Jupiter. (The city of Arezzo was so famous for its bronzes in antiquity that the German word for metal, Erz, was derived from its name.) In Greece, in the early period, votive figures of gods and humans bore inscriptions scratched or engraved on their bodies, but the custom soon died out. In Etruria, and elsewhere in Italy under Etruscan influence, it survived, along with other Archaic forms and features. Some of the finest Etruscan statues and statuettes of the Classical period and later bear inscriptions carved into their mantles, on their bodies, or on their armour; for example the Arringatore in Florence and the Mars from Todi (Umbrian in language, Etruscan in style).

Other metals used include gold, silver and lead. On the three famous gold tablets from 5
Pyrgi – in spite of their delicate appearance they are heavy plaques – the text is engraved in the soft gold surface and there are traces of words erased and written over. (A bronze tablet was also found with these.) The gold tablets were originally attached, perhaps to the wall of a temple; the nail holes, and some golden nails used for this purpose, are still extant. A gold *bulla* (pendant) has a relief design of a flying Daedalus and his son Icarus. Incised inscriptions identify the two: *taitle,* 'Daedalus' and *vikare,* 'Icarus'.

A cheap substitute for more expensive materials was lead, which had the added advantage of being soft and easy to write on. It was often used to make inexpensive religious or votive figures. Curses were written on lead tablets by Greeks, Etruscans, Romans and other peoples in ancient Italy. These so-called *tabulae defixionis* bore prayers, incantations and magic formulas designed to harm or incapacitate enemies and rivals. The tablets were rolled up and 'posted' in someone's tomb, for the Underworld. Lead was also used for inscriptions, such as a ribbon-like tablet from a sanctuary near Santa Marinella and a thin round plate from Magliano, with ritual, probably funerary, inscriptions (see p. 28). Epitaphs were incised on stone sarcophagi, cippi, urns, stelai and tombs, or painted in the rock-cut tombs of Tarquinia.

Inscriptions on coins and gems are short, but important. Etruscan coins, made of gold, 40 silver and bronze, were usually struck by dies (as coins are today); sometimes they were cast in moulds. Only a few issues carry 'legends' (inscriptions) or other symbols to identify their origin.

Gems, like mirrors, provide 'picture bilinguals': inscription and image explain each
22–8 other. Some 3,000 gems have survived, but not all are inscribed. They are often extremely beautiful and provide important information about religion, mythology and language. Single figures, shown bending over to fit the rounded frame, or more rarely in groups, are labelled with names of Greek mythological characters: Achle (Achilles); the Trojan hero Paris; Taitle (Daidalos); Easun (Jason); Hercle or Herkle (Herakles). A gem
9 in the Bibliothèque Nationale with a youth reading the numbers written on a pair of tablets has the word *apcar,* which is Etruscan for *abacus,* the Latin word for a counting-board (*b* becomes *p* in Etruscan). Their great number is due to the fact that they were widely used as jewellery (rather than only to seal documents and containers by impressing the bezel of the ring into soft wax or clay). Like mirrors, they belonged to the luxurious world of wealthy Etruscans, who adorned themselves not only for pleasure but as a way of showing their status in society.

9 A gem showing a youth reading numbers from a tablet, *c.*450 BC (*TLE* 779). Paris, Bibliothèque Nationale.

4
Etruscan Inscriptions

Etruscan inscriptions – on stone, lead, clay, bronze, tomb walls, etc. – total about 13,000; a very large number if we consider how few we have for the other ancient non-Latin languages of Italy. Eleven inscriptions describing a religious ritual, the bronze Iguvine tablets from Gubbio – written partly in an Etruscan, partly in a Latin alphabet – are almost all that remains of the pre-Roman Umbrian language; a few hundred in Venetic and Oscan have come down to us; only three inscriptions in the Gauls' language, and none in the indigenous dialects of Sardinia and Corsica. The Faliscan language is attested by about 150 inscriptions; a large number, due to the close ties of Falerii with the literate Etruscan culture. In archaic Latin we have only nine inscriptions earlier than the third century BC, including one new one, and one, the Praenestine fibula, said to be a forgery.

Most of the 13,000 Etruscan inscriptions (more are continually being discovered) can be understood. Most are pitifully short. The majority are funerary inscriptions, consisting only of the name of the deceased, the patronymic, or father's name, sometimes the matronymic, or mother's name, and the surname or family name. What would be known of the English language if there were hardly anything but tombstones and other short inscriptions to read?

Longer inscriptions

The few long texts that have come down to us are described briefly below.

The Zagreb mummy

The longest and most exotic Etruscan inscription which survives is a religious text, a sacred linen book, parts of which were preserved by being used as linen wrappings on a mummy. The mummy, that of a 30-year old woman, was bought in Egypt by a Croatian traveller in the last century and given to the Zagreb National Museum in Yugoslavia, where it remains today. When the wrappings were removed from the body they were found to contain a neatly inked text of some 1,200 readable words, in at least twelve vertical columns. It was a liturgical calendar of sacrifices and prayers to be made to a number of gods, for instance Nethuns (Neptune), on specific dates. Though damaged and spotted by the unguents used for mummification, and largely unintelligible because of its technical vocabulary and the repetitions typical of religious texts, it is uniquely precious for our knowledge of the Etruscan language. A typical passage runs (column VIII, lines 3ff.): *celi* (the month of September) *huthis zathrumis* (the 26th [day]) *flerchva* (all the offerings) *nethunsl* (to the god Neptune) *sucri* (should be declared) *thezri-c* (and should be made).

The Capua tile

On a terracotta tile from Capua in Campania, dating from the fifth or fourth century BC, now in the State Museum in East Berlin, is incised a long funerary ritual, honouring the gods of the Underworld. Sixty-two lines are preserved, with almost 300 legible words. Among the gods mentioned are Calus, Laruns, Lethams, Tinia, Uni, and perhaps Bacchus.

The Santa Marinella lead sheet
On both sides of a lead sheet found in fragments during the 1964–5 excavations at a sanctuary near Santa Marinella, not far from Pyrgi, is a much damaged inscription, with very small letters. It is today in the Villa Giulia Museum, Rome. Several words are similar to those found on the Zagreb mummy cloth and the Capua tile; this too was evidently a religious document. It contains traces of 80 or more words, half of which can be read, and dates from the fifth century BC.

The Magliano plaque
The text of a lens-shaped lead plaque found at Magliano, in the Albegna river valley (now in the Archaeological Museum in Florence), contains some 70 words running in a spiral from the exterior inward to the centre. It was written during the fifth century BC, and mentions the gods Calus, Suri (Apollo Soranus?), Cautha, Maris, Thanr and Tins; the word for 'gods', *aiseras,* also occurs. The text seems to have been funerary in nature.

The Pyrgi tablets (Fig. 5)
Shorter, but very important because of their historical implications and because they provide us with the closest thing to a bilingual inscription, are the texts inscribed on the three gold tablets found at Pyrgi, the harbour of Caere (Cerveteri), in 1964. (Because of their great value they are kept in a bank vault in Rome. Reproductions are on view in the Villa Giulia Museum). Two are in Etruscan, one in Phoenician. A fourth tablet, in bronze and fragmentary, also had an Etruscan inscription, mentioning the goddess of dawn, Thesan. The tablets date from about 500 BC. The longest Etruscan text, which has 16 lines and 36 (or 37) words, parallels the Phoenician text but does not provide a word-for-word translation: it is no Rosetta Stone. It gives a free translation of the text of a dedication by the ruler of Cisra (Caere), Thefarie Velianas, as a thank-offering to the goddess Uni, identified as Astarte (*Štrt*) in the Phoenician text. *Turce* is translated in the Phoenician inscription as 'gave'; *zilac* is 'king' (*mlk); ci* is 'three'. The goddess 'held him in her hand three years' (*ci avil* = three years).

The Perugia cippus
A later (second or first century BC) inscription on a stone *cippus* or boundary-marker from Perugia (in the Perugia Museum) bears on two sides a finely carved text of 46 lines and 130 words. This was a property contract between members of the Velthina and Afuna families. The word *tular,* 'boundary' or 'boundaries', features prominently among the legal formulas and repetitions.

The epitaph of Laris Pulena
The epitaph of Laris Pulena of Tarquinia (Tarquinia Museum) is engraved on a representation of a long strip of cloth (the *volumen* of the Romans). Half-unrolled in the hands of its owner, it is proudly displayed by the deceased, who reclines on his stone sarcophagus as if on a couch. The 9 lines and 59 words can in large part be interpreted by comparing the text with the Latin *elogia* (honorary epitaphs) of the Scipios at Rome.

The Piacenza liver (Fig. 10)
An unusual document, providing invaluable evidence for Etruscan divination, is a bronze model of a sheep's liver which was discovered in 1877 near Piacenza in northern Italy (Museo Civico, Piacenza). Because of peculiarities of script and spelling, scholars think it was made near Chiusi about 150 BC. On the outer margin it is divided into sixteen regions, reflecting the sections of the sky; there are in addition twenty-four regions on the interior of the liver and two on the underside. It gives fifty-two names of divinities, mostly abbreviated. Many are repeated. Some of these are known from other sources: *tin* = Jupiter, *uni* = Juno, *catha* = a sun god, *cel* = a mother goddess, *selvan* = Silvanus, *fufluns* = Bacchus, *hercle* = Hercules, *usil* = the sun, *tivr* = the moon. Many of the divinities are local Italic gods. Hercle, Fufluns, Usil, Uni and Tin are also represented and labelled on the backs of bronze mirrors, as is *celsclan,* 'son of Cel', who appears as a giant, son of Mother Earth.

10 Bronze model of a sheep's liver, from Piacenza, *c.* 150 BC (*TLE* 719).

Short inscriptions

Shorter inscriptions occur on mirrors and gems, vases, tableware, sarcophagi and urns, votive figures and coins.

Mirrors
The engraved decoration on Etruscan bronze mirrors contrasts with the three-dimensional decoration and supports of most Greek mirrors. The Etruscan examples provide us with a continuous series of line drawings, and often inscriptions, from the Archaic to the later Hellenistic period (*c.* 530–200 BC). They were produced in various Etruscan cities, but since such small luxury objects were given as gifts and widely exported, in ancient as well as in modern times, it is difficult to establish their provenance and to recognise the workshops where they were made.

Mirrors were probably given to women at their weddings or on other special occasions. Like most surviving luxury objects, they were found in the graves of their owners, who took their precious possessions with them. So far, mirrors have been found in women's tombs only. Inscriptions also make it clear that the mirrors were made for women, as on one which Tite Cale gave to his mother (*ati*):

> *tite cale:atial:turce:malstria:cver*
> 'Tite Cale to his mother gave this mirror as a gift'.

The sense of *cver* as a sacred object, like the Greek *agalma,* suggests that the mirror was dedicated to his dead mother, to take to the tomb.

Another mirror, from Sentinum in Umbria, says,

mi malena larthia puruhenas, 'I [am] the mirror of Larthia Puruhena'.

These two inscriptions give us the Etruscan words for 'mirror', *malstria* and *malena*, with
11 the characteristic ending in *-na.* Another, in the British Museum, says:

mi thancvilus fulnial, 'I [am the mirror] of Thancvil Fulni'.

11 Bronze mirror belonging to Thancvil Fulni, with a man and a woman talking, *c.* 300 BC. Diam. *c.* 16 cm (BM Br 724, 1868.5–20.55; *TLE* 749).

12 Bronze mirror from Chiusi, 3rd century BC, inscribed *śuthina*. Diam. 12.5 cm (BM Br 722, 1873.8–20.106).

12 Once dedicated to the grave, some were inscribed with the formula *śuthina* scratched on the reflecting surface so as to preclude their re-use or theft.

Most inscriptions on mirrors, however, are of mythological names, often Etruscan transcriptions and transformations of the names of Greek mythological figures, many of which were known in Etruria from the plays of the Greek tragedians and their followers. Other names of heroes and gods bring us close to Etruscan religion, literature and even history. The broad range of subjects depicted includes remarkable examples of local interpretations of Greek myths and legends, and local types. A popular figure in Etruria, Hercle, or Herkle, the Etruscan Herakles, was introduced quite early to central Italy,

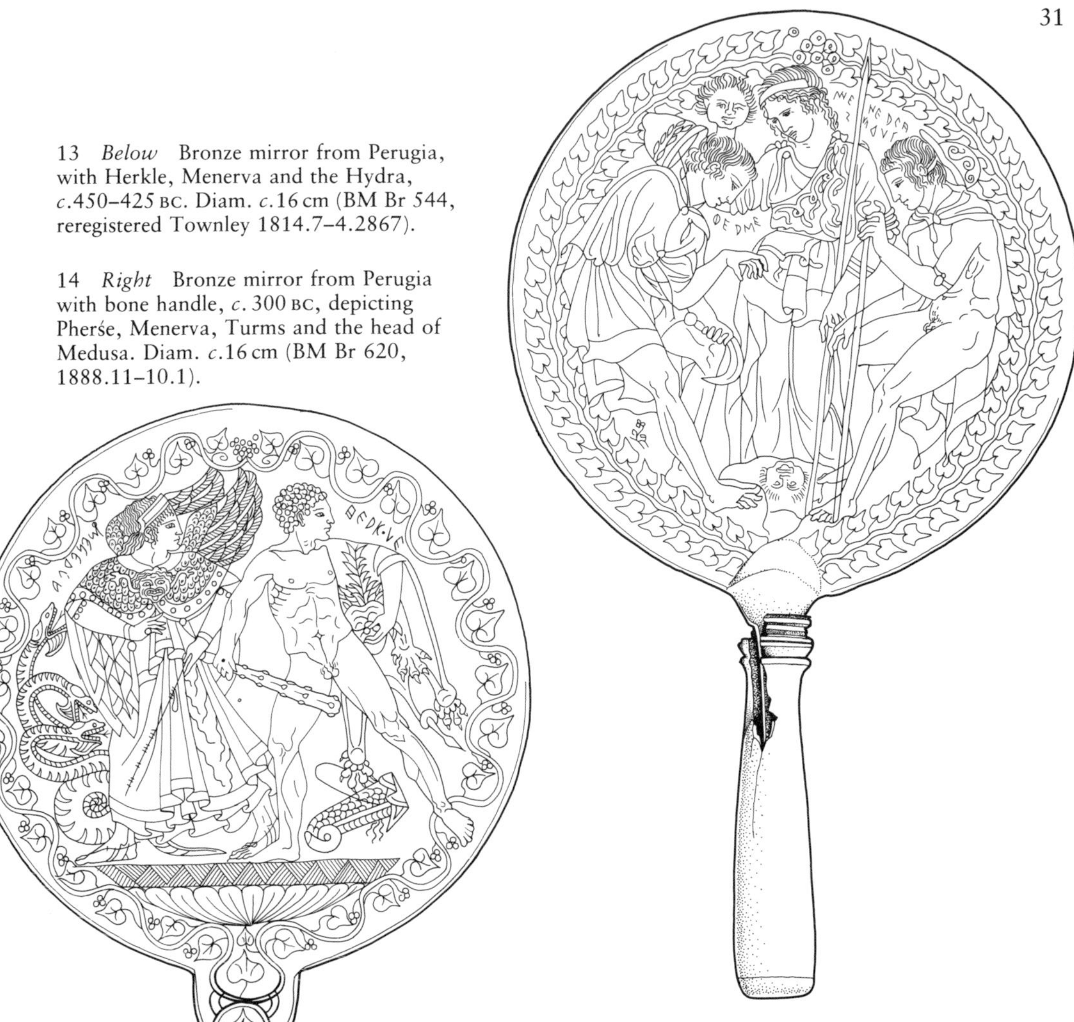

13 *Below* Bronze mirror from Perugia, with Herkle, Menerva and the Hydra, *c.*450–425 BC. Diam. *c.*16 cm (BM Br 544, reregistered Townley 1814.7–4.2867).

14 *Right* Bronze mirror from Perugia with bone handle, *c.* 300 BC, depicting Pherśe, Menerva, Turms and the head of Medusa. Diam. *c.*16 cm (BM Br 620, 1888.11–10.1).

probably as Herakles Melqart, the Phoenician hero. He is shown on numerous mirrors,
including an example in the British Museum's collection, dating from about 450–425 BC,
accompanied by his divine patron and frequent companion, the goddess Menerva (this is 13
the Archaic, unsyncopated form of her name; the Latin form of her name is Minerva).
Menerva also appears on a mirror (about 300 BC) with another protégé, Pherśe (Perseus).
Also shown is Turms, the god Hermes, who has lent Pherśe the cap of invisibility, here
shown hanging down his back. All three gaze at the reflected image – appropriate for a 14
mirror – of the decapitated Medusa, whose head Menerva holds up. Here, as elsewhere,
the names are fitted into the spaces left blank by the design's composition. The direction
of the writing follows the personages labelled: Pherse's and Menerva's names run left to
right, starting from their images; Turms' starts near his head, on the right, and runs
leftward.

On an ambitious mirror from Bolsena, the characters in the central scene are identified 15
by inscriptions around the outer margins (a feature typical of a later series of mirrors).
Menrva is shown in full regalia – crested, flowing-maned helmet, Gorgon-headed aegis,
and spear: yet her role is that of a *kourotrophos,* the Greek word for a deity holding a

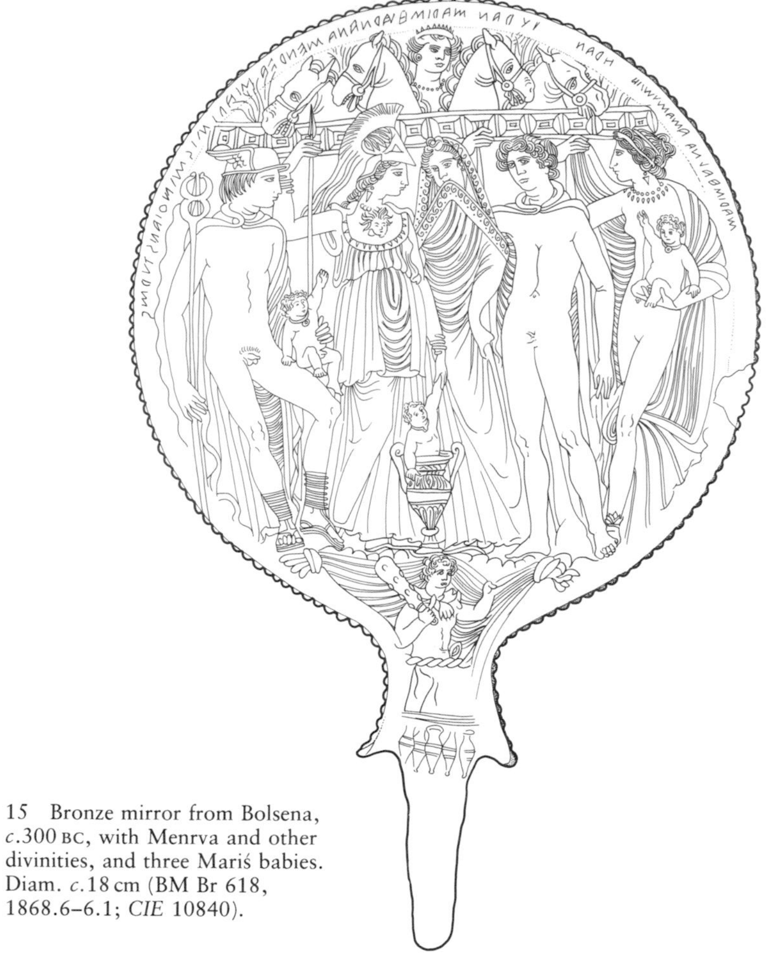

15 Bronze mirror from Bolsena, *c.*300 BC, with Menrva and other divinities, and three Mariś babies. Diam. *c.*18 cm (BM Br 618, 1868.6–6.1; *CIE* 10840).

child. With her left hand she holds or pulls a child, Mariś Husrnana, out of a volute *krater*. Next to her stands Turan, the goddess of love. She is not naked, as often, but tightly wrapped in a handsomely bordered mantle which she holds up to her mouth so that only her upper face is seen. (She is dressed in a similar manner on a mirror showing Helen and Menelaos, and may represent a goddess of marriage.) Laran (the 'L' is obliterated), hand on spear, watches the scene. Two side figures, Turms (Hermes) on the left and the female Amamtunia, hold two other children: Mariś Isminthians (on Turms' knee) and Mariś Halna (on Amamtunia's left arm).

On another mirror, from Chiusi, with a similar scene, Menrva has bared her breast as though to nurse a child and holds Mariś Husrnana with both hands. Turan helps her, while Leinth (not Turms) holds another baby on his left knee. An unidentified fourth figure has the pose, *chlamys* and spear of Laran on the Bolsena mirror. Both mirrors, and a Praenestine cista or toilet box, showing Menrva helping an adult Mariś who is rising out of a huge jar, represent indigenous scenes. Mariś is not Mars, but a local divinity who, according to one interpretation, lived for the considerable period of 130 years, and had three lives. The scene on the Bolsena mirror, in connection with the others on which he appears, has been interpreted as showing Mariś' birth, life and death. There is no general scholarly agreement, but a number of interesting possibilities are worth con-

16 Bronze mirror from Chiusi, late 4th century BC, with Fufluns, his wife Areatha, his mother Semla and a satyr. Diam. *c.*21 cm (BM Br 630, 1847.11–1.21).

sideration. Husrnana, perhaps connected with *husiur,* 'children' (with a double suffix, *-na-na*) may refer to Mariś birth as the 'baby boy'. Various possible connections have been suggested for *halna,* an epithet which would refer to the living, or mature Mariś. Finally, Mariś Isminthians, whose epithet seems related to that of Apollo Smintheus, would represent Mariś' encounter with death: the baby is held by Turms, as Hermes or Mercury Psychopompus, guide of souls to the Underworld, on the Bolsena mirror. Leinth, whose name is connected to *lein,* 'death', holds Mariś on the other mirror. The three babies might be the children of Menrva and Hercle.

Fufluns (Dionysos, Bacchus, Liber) was an important Etruscan divinity, whose name
appears on the Piacenza liver. On a handsome mirror of the late fourth century BC, a 16
young Fufluns is shown with his partner Areatha (Ariadne). He holds a swan-headed lyre. The divine couple, formed, as often in Etruscan art, of an older woman and a young man, is flanked by Fufluns' mother Semla (Semele) and a Dionysiac reveler, a pug-nosed, animal-eared satyr named Sime, 'snub-nosed'. The lush, stylised trumpet flowers of the border betray an influence from the south, possibly from Apulian vases.

17 Bronze mirror with toilet scene, late 4th century BC. Diam. 20 cm (BM Br 626, 1865.1–3.39).

Helen, not surprisingly (given her legendary reputation for beauty), was a favourite subject for Etruscan mirror-makers and often appears in toilet and adornment scenes.
17 One mirror, dating from the fourth century BC (all the figures are still dressed in heavy drapery rather than appearing in the graceful nudity preferred in the Hellenistic period), shows Malavisch dressing. Malavisch may be an Etruscan name or epithet for Helen, meaning something akin to 'the one adorned' and related to *malstria* and *malena,* both meaning 'mirror'. Assisting her are four female figures, depicted in the solemn, majestic style of the fourth century: Turan, Munthuch, Zipu and Hinthial. These names, too, have been connected with adornment scenes. *Hinthial,* 'ghost', 'shade', 'reflection', one of the most intriguing and important words in Etruscan, may, however, refer to the 'shade of Helen'. The fourth-century BC Tomb of Orcus in Tarquinia represents the shades, *hinthial*, of Teriasals (Teiresias) and [Ach]memrun (Agamemnon), and a contemporary Etruscan vase shows the *hinthial* of two Amazons, Turmuca (perhaps Aturmuca, Andromache) and Pentasila (Penthesilea).

Belief in the importance of divination and omens played an important role in Etruscan

18 Bronze mirror from Bolsena, *c.*300 BC, with Cacu, Artile and the Vipinas brothers. Diam. 15 cm (BM Br 633, 1873.8–20.105; *CIE* 10854). *Below* Detail of the inscription on the tablet.

tradition and may lie behind another remarkable mirror in the British Museum. Like the Mariś mirror, it comes from the Bolsena region. This third-century mirror is justly known as an example of Etruscan historical art, for it depicts a local myth or legend and records names known to us from Roman historical tradition. Two youths are seated in a sylvan landscape, indicated by the background as well as by the head of a satyr. Cacu plays a lyre; Artile reads from a hinged diptych, on which are inscribed some letters, impossible to decipher. Cacu, the Latin Cacus, is here a seer; thus his Apollo-like appearance. Artile, a boy, seems to be reading a prophecy. Two figures approach in a stealthy manner; their names, inscribed on the margin of the mirror, reveal that they are the brothers Caile Vipinas and Aule Vipinas, known to the Romans as Caeles and Aulus Vibenna. Roman historians place the story of Caeles Vibenna – whose name was remembered in the Caelian Hill in Rome – in the time of the Tarquins, the late sixth century BC. 18

A homogeneous group of later mirrors, dating from the Hellenistic period (third

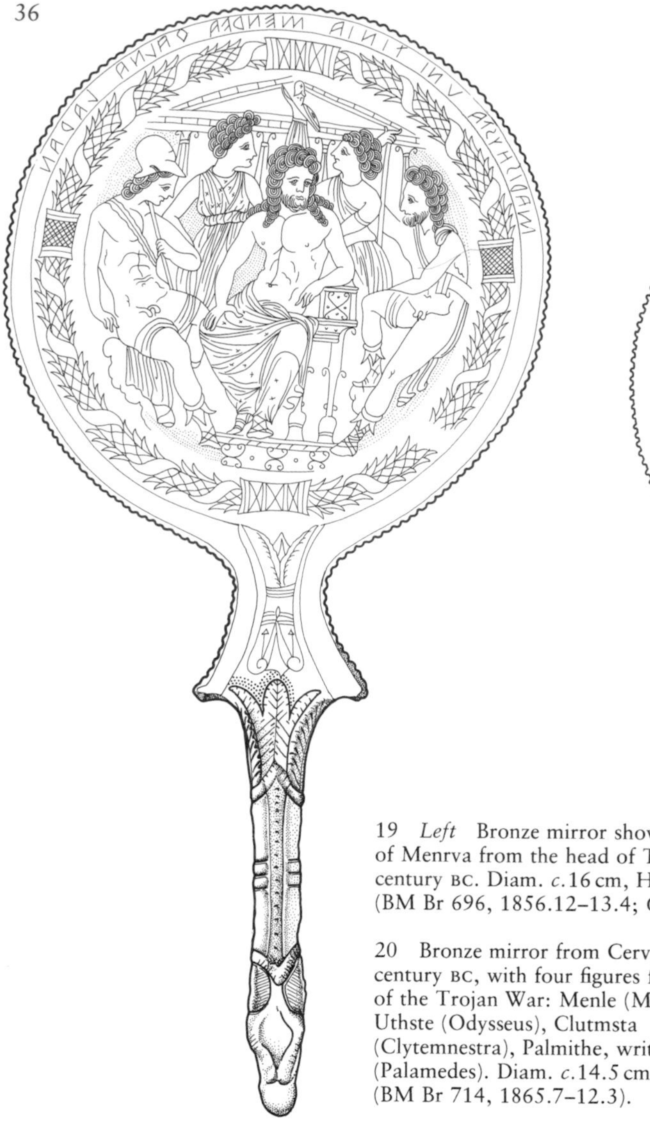

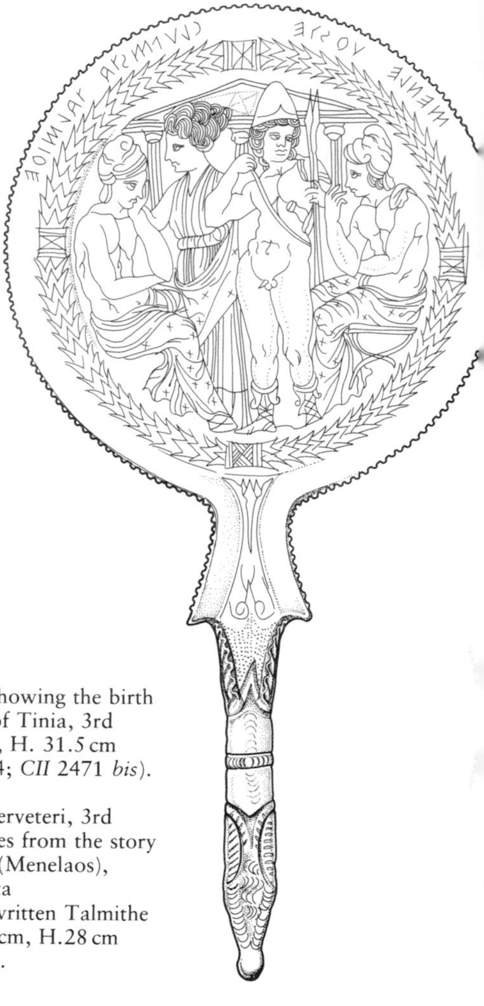

19 *Left* Bronze mirror showing the birth of Menrva from the head of Tinia, 3rd century BC. Diam. *c.*16 cm, H. 31.5 cm (BM Br 696, 1856.12–13.4; *CII* 2471 *bis*).

20 Bronze mirror from Cerveteri, 3rd century BC, with four figures from the story of the Trojan War: Menle (Menelaos), Uthste (Odysseus), Clutmsta (Clytemnestra), Palmithe, written Talmithe (Palamedes). Diam. *c.*14.5 cm, H.28 cm (BM Br 714, 1865.7–12.3).

century BC) are characterised by a number of features: (1) a border decoration in the form of a spiky garland, often fastened at the top, bottom and side, sometimes ending in two pine cones; (2) the frequent presence of the word *śuthina* scratched on the reflecting surface; (3) the use of the outer, plain border as a field for the inscriptions identifying the characters represented; (4) a cast handle terminating in a ram's head; (5) hair-styles shown as neatly arranged concentric circles; and (6) a standard size, usually 13–14 cm in diameter. They were evidently made in the same workshop, perhaps at Orvieto. Other features, such as the presence of the god Laran or 'conversation groups' of four gracefully lounging figures, characterise some, though not all, mirrors in this group.

The British Museum has several of these 'Spiky Garland' mirrors. One shows the birth
19 of Menrva from the head of her father Tinia (Zeus, Jupiter), in the presence of four divinities: Laran, Thalna (a nymph), Uni (Tinia's wife) and Maris Tiusta, bearded like Tinia. The circumstances are unlike any we know of from Greek myth: Uni and Thalna

assist Tinia; but the presence of a martial god, Laran, perhaps identified with Mars, and of the Italic god Maris, seem to refer to local stories unknown to us from literature.

Two other Spiky Garland mirrors show characters from the Trojan War. In one, a 'conversation group' of four figures, are included two seated male figures on the sides, labelled Talmithe, for Palmithe (Palamedes, here written with a *t* instead of a *p*), and 20
Menle. In the centre stand Clutmsta, Clytemnestra (perhaps written *clupmsta,* with a *p* instead of a *t*) and Uthste, Odysseus (the *delta,* Δ, of the Greek is reproduced by O, *theta*). What story did the artist or craftsman have in mind when he showed Clytemnestra, Odysseus, Menelaos and Palamedes together? There were certainly Etruscan versions of Greek myths, and more versions of 'Trojan' stories than we perhaps know of. Menle and Talmithe wear Phrygian hats usually reserved for Easterners, Trojans, or the divine twins Castur and Pultuce (Castor and Pollux). On this inexpensive mirror, we may have stock figures from a standard repertoire of models, labelled with names picked at will. Books of such models may have been available in workshops of the Hellenistic period, when mirrors and relief-decorated funerary urns were practically mass-produced.

The second mirror represents an animated scene perhaps harking back to a theatrical performance. Troilos, 21
the youngest of Priam's fifty sons, was killed and decapitated by a bloodthirsty Achilles, Achle, shown in the centre of the mirror with fellow-warrior Evas (Ajax). Achilles rests his knee on an altar after savagely murdering the boy. On the border of the altar is engraved Troilos' name, Truil(e), beside which, we realise with a shock, is the huge cadaver of the horse on which Troilos rode down from Priam's high place, into the ambush of Achilles. To the right stands Echtur, Achilles' mortal enemy, Hector (who would die later by Achilles' hand). The winged female demon on the left, Vanth, is a purely Etruscan divinity.

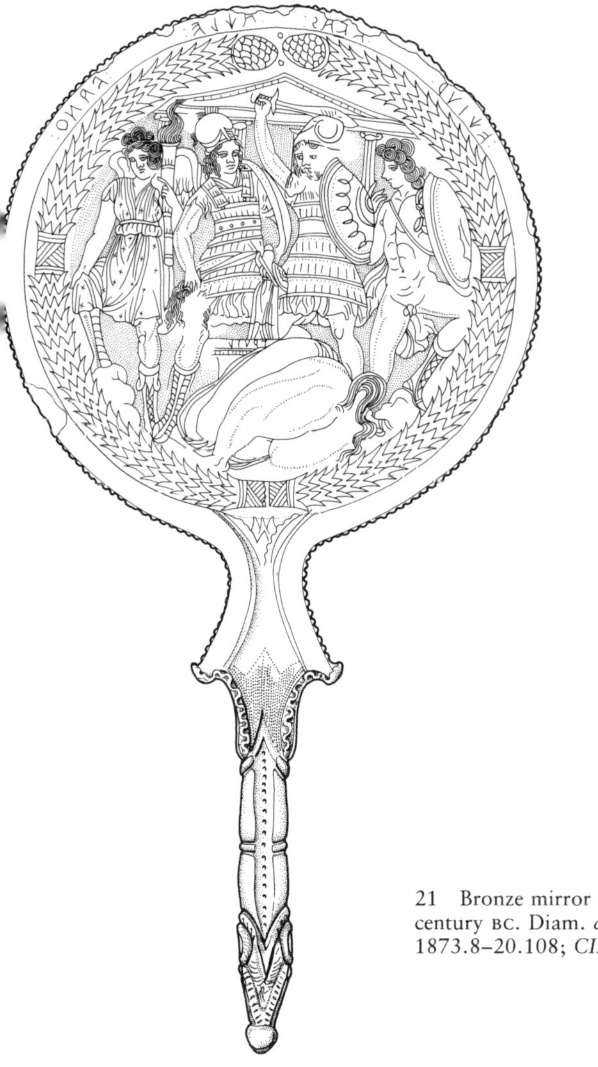

21 Bronze mirror with the death of Truile (Troilos), 3rd century BC. Diam. *c.*16 cm, H. 31 cm (BM Br 625, 1873.8–20.108; *CIE* 10862).

22 Hercle resting, c.400 BC. H.1.6 cm (BM Gem 769, 1814.7–4.1299).

23 Herkle and Kukne, 5th century BC. 15 × 11 mm (BM Gem 621, 1867.5–7.335).

24 Achle in retirement, 500–400 BC, 14 × 11 mm (BM Gem 632, 1867.5–7.414).

Engraved gems

One of the most characteristic and beautiful Etruscan gems in the British Museum,
22 perhaps from Chiusi, bears a design with the stooped figure of Hercle (Hercules) sitting
on a rock. Beside him is the lion skin. The letters of his name follow the curve of his arm,
head and shoulder, filling in the blank space in a pleasing design. Hercules is by far the
most popular figure on Etruscan gems. His name appears spelled either Hercle, as here,
or Herkle, as on a remarkable late Archaic gem, showing him in action, lunging against
23 his enemy Kukne or Cycnus. Here the name, written almost vertically, nicely fills the
space behind the hero's back and muscular thighs, in the Archaic style.

Also very popular was Achilles, whose name appears variously as Achale, Achele,
Achile, or in its syncopated form, Achle, as on a cornelian scarab from Tarquinia. The
24 scene reminds us of his retirement from battle in the *Iliad.*

The Trojans occupied a special place in Etruscan myth (the later Romans, of course,
thought of Aeneas as their founder). So it is not surprising to find a sardonyx gem in the
25 Classical style representing the Trojan hero Paris as an archer, as he is described by
Homer. Here again, the widely spaced letters of his name fill the empty spaces, following
the course of the gem's border, with its characteristic dot pattern.

The craftsman Taitle, or Daedalus, appears three times on Etruscan jewellery of the
fifth century BC: twice on gems and once on a golden *bulla,* where he is shown along with
his son, Vikare (Icarus), and with his saw and adze. The British Museum gem illustrates
26 their tragic voyage. Taitle's name is neatly written in a horizontal line above the hooked
signs which represent the waves of the sea over which he soars.

Easun (Jason) is shown embarking on the ship *Argo,* whose furnishings or fittings fill
27 the space all around the figure. The letters of his name are fitted in on either side of his legs
and along the side of the cornelian bezel. The relatively free field of another gem, in
28 contrast, is filled with the bold lettering of the Etruscan name given to a bearded,
powerful, striding male figure: Tarchnas. He holds jumping weights, and so may be an
athlete. Perhaps, however, this personal name, so common in Etruria, is the name of the
owner.

25 Paris the archer, late 5th century BC. H.1.5 cm (BM Gem 631, 1772.3–15.475).

26 Taitle flying over the sea, 450–400 BC. H.c.1.6 cm (BM Gem 663, 1772.3–15.366).

27 Easun by his ship, late 5th century BC. 16 × 12 mm (BM Gem 669, 1872.6–4.1166).

28 Tarchnas as athlete, with jumping weights, 500–470 BC. 13 × 10 mm (BM Gem 643, 1849.6–23.5).

Vases

The Etruscans imported huge quantities of Greek vases and adopted the Greek names for them, as surviving inscriptions show. A *kylix* will bear an inscription saying, *mi chulichna (culichna,* or *culchna),* 'I am the culichna', or *kylix.* Another cup says: *mi qutun karkanas,* 'I am the *kothon* of Karkana'. An oil jar is a *lechtumuza,* 'little *lekythos*', or *aska eleivana,* 'leather container (*aska*) for oil (*eleivana*)'. Etruscan *thina* derives from Greek *dinos,* a type of bowl; *ulpaia* from Greek *olpe; pruchum* from Greek *prochous.* Other names of vases are native Etruscan: *thafna, zavena,* the latter an indigenous Etruscan shape, the ancestor of the Greek *kantharos.*

29 Perfume vase of Velthur Hathiśna, in the form of a lion. From Veii, 7th century BC. H.6.5 cm (BM Terracotta 1683, 1852.1–12.8; *CII* 2561).

An early (seventh to sixth century BC) impasto (rough terracotta) perfume vase in the
form of a reclining (couchant) lion, about 10 cm long, was found at Veii and is now in the 29
British Museum. Below the left ear runs the vertical inscription:

velthur hathi ξ naṣ

The owner's name is given in the genitive case: '(I am the vase [or, 'I am the possession']) of Velthur Hathiśna'. Here the genitive ending *-s* is added only to the last name, Hathiśna. The form of the internal *s,* a five-bar (ξ) sigma, instead of the more usual three-bar sigma, testifies to its early date. The owner of the vase has a typically Etruscan name. Velthur is a common first name, while Hathiśna has the characteristically Etruscan ending in *-na,* as in Porsenna, Rasna, Karkana, Tarchna (Tarquin), etc. In small or more primitive societies an individual was easily identified by his or her first name, with the simple addition of the father's name, or patronymic. As society became more complex and cities developed, people needed a second name: a gentilicial, or family name (this name often developed from an original patronymic, like O'Connor or McDonald). So the appearance of the family (*gens*) name, recognisable by its adjectival form, with a *-na* ending, is a mark of the newly urbanised Etruscan society.

Another very early inscription is on a bucchero *kantharos,* or two-handled drinking 30
cup. In the seventh and sixth centuries BC, such bucchero cups were exported from Etruria all over the Mediterranean, from Corinth to Carthage and beyond. The shape, typical of Etruria, was adopted by the Greeks, who represented it in the hand of the wine

30 Bucchero *kantharos* (drinking cup) of Avile Repesuna, *c.*600 BC. H. *c.*12 cm (BM 1953.4–26.1; *TLE* 765).

god Dionysos himself. The words, scratched on the smooth buffed black surface, again indicate ownership. The object speaks in the first person,

mi repesunas aviles 'I [am] of Repesuna Avile', that is, 'I belong to Avile Repesuna'.

The verb 'to be' (*am*) can be omitted, as in Greek and Latin and in Indo-European languages generally. The ending *-s* indicates the genitive case, which also functions as a dative. *Avile* is a common first name; it can sometimes, as here, follow the name of the *gens*, or family name. *Repesuna* again has the characteristic Etruscan ending *-na.*

Another drinking vessel, a *rhyton* in the shape of a mule's head, dating from the fifth
31 century BC, also has connections with the drinking party or *symposium,* a Greek social function which the Etruscans adopted as a sign of civilisation. A *rhyton,* a kind of party cup or drinking horn, does not have a flat base, so it could not be put down until emptied. Scholars are divided as to whether the craftsman who made this example was Greek or Etruscan. There is no doubt about the inscription, however. It is Etruscan:

fuflunl pachies velclthi 'of [to] Fufluns Bacchus, at Vulci'.

The god to whom the cup was dedicated is the Etruscan Fufluns, known from numerous mirrors as well as two gold *bullae* and the Piacenza liver. Here, his name is written

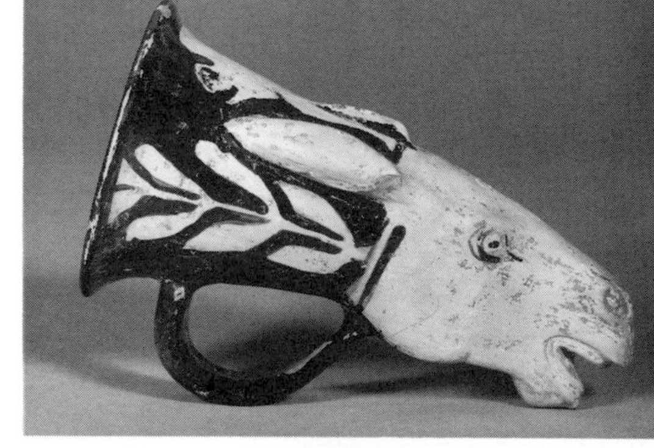

31 *Rhyton* (drinking horn) in the shape of a mule's head, dedicated to Fufluns Bacchus. From Vulci, 5th century BC. H.19.25 cm (BM Vase F489, 1837.6–9.79; *TLE* 336). *Below* Detail of the inscription on the handle.

without the final *-s,* and with the genitive *-l. Pachies* is the Etruscan transcription of the Greek name Baccheios, a cultic epithet of the Greek Dionysos. This double name has been compared to the double name of Uni Astre in the Pyrgi tablet, where it is likewise found in the genitive, *unial astres* (both *-al* and *-s* are genitive forms). Two other fifth-century BC vase inscriptions may document the growing influence of the cult of Dionysos, or Bacchus (also known as Liber in Italy), and his identification with the local god Fufluns. Much later, in the second century, we find reference to the cult of a god Pacha, not only on the Piacenza liver, but on three sarcophagi as well. On that of Laris Pulena, they are mentioned together. On another epitaph, Lars Statlane is said to be *maru* (a magistrate) of Catha and Pacha (*cathas pachanac:* the ending *-c,* similar to the Latin enclitic *-que,* means 'and'). Most interesting is the locative *velclthi,* 'at Vulci' (*-thi* is the sign of the locative) appearing on all three inscriptions. It has been convincingly compared to other locatives of cities, *tarchnalthi (TLE* 131,174). 'at Tarquinia', and *velsnalthi (TLE* 902), 'at Volsinii'.

32 A later vase has the letters scratched into its black glaze so that they show up by contrast in the light pink of the clay beneath. Carefully and boldly incised all around the widest part of the pot, they form an effective decoration of its plain black-glazed surface and highlight its shape. To be noted are the extremely long stroke used to render the *i* of *Fastis* at the centre of the inscription, and the two dots used to separate the words. The vase is quite tall (20 cm) and comes from Arezzo. This handsome inscription is easy to read:

32 'Black-glaze' vase of Larthia Levei, from Arezzo, 3rd century BC. H.20 cm (BM 1946.10–12.1; *CIE* 4639).

> *larthia levei fastis aneinal sec*
> 'Larthia Levei, of Fasti Aneina, the daughter', that is, 'Larthia Levei, daughter of Fasti Aneina'.

Larthia's names have the typical feminine endings in *-a* and *-i* in the nominative form. She is identified as the daughter of Fasti Aneina, as we see from the genitive endings *-s* and *-l.* This is an unusual inscription, even in Etruria where women had more independence than in Greece or Rome, but were normally identified by reference to their fathers (as daughter, *sec*) or husbands (as wife, *puia*).

Bronze tableware

Several groups of inscribed bronze tableware once buried with their wealthy owners can now be studied in the British Museum. They were all made around 300 BC, but may have been buried later as heirlooms. Such wine and banqueting services consisted of pitchers, bowls, buckets, strainers and ladles, for use at the feasts, banquets and *symposia* of Etruscan nobles. When the owners died, some of these objects were inscribed with their names, followed by the usual formula *śuthina,* signifying that they were dedicated to their graves, for their use in the Underworld. Often objects were simply marked *śuthina.*

A fragmentary bronze mirror and nine vases remain from a tomb group originally consisting of fourteen bronze serving pieces, found in 1865 at Castel Giorgio near Orvieto. The tomb belonged to a man, Larth Metie, and a woman, indicated by the presence of the mirror. Two wine jugs and three buckets with handles are inscribed (on
33 one some of the letters are corroded). One of the buckets, or *situlae,* is particularly beautiful, decorated with relief heads of Menrva and of a satyr, whose large open mouth (with built-in strainer) was the spout, inscribed:

larth meties śuthina, 'Of Larth Metie, for the tomb'.

The genitive ending *-s* occurs only on the last name.

33 Bronze situla and wine jug from near Orvieto, part of the tomb group of Larth Metie, late 4th century BC. H.29.5 cm (BM Br 652–3, 1873.8–20.202 and 204; *TLE* 216, *CIE* 10876, 78).

A large bronze wine and banqueting service from nearby Bolsena is divided between the British Museum and the Museo Gregoriano in the Vatican. The two pieces in the
34 British Museum are inscribed with the owner's name:

larisal havrenieś śuthina, 'Of Laris [Lars] Havrenie, for the tomb'.

34 Inscription from a bronze wine crater, part of Laris Havrenie's tomb group from Bolsena, 350–300 BC (BM Br 651, cf. 655, 1868.6–6.5, cf.2; *TLE* 210, *CIE* 10830–31).

Of note are the two genitive endings *-al* and *-ś*. One piece has the letter *A* below the inscription: it is hard to tell what it stood for.

Part of another tomb group from Bolsena is also in the British Museum. The handsome bronze grave furnishings were dedicated to a woman: they included the important mirror showing the ambush of the Vipinas brothers. An incense burner (*thymiaterion*) is decorated with figures of a boy, a cat catching a bird, a rooster, and – on the basin – four birds. The inscription names the tomb's owner,

thania lucini śuthina, 'Of Thania Lucini, for the tomb'.

The name in the nominative with *śuthina* is unusual.

Sarcophagi and ash urns

Names of Etruscan men and women also occur on epitaphs, coffins and ash urns once in family tombs. An impressive terracotta sarcophagus from Chiusi (approx. 180 × 120 cm) dates from the Hellenistic period, about 150 BC. Reclining on the lid, as if on a comfortable banqueting couch, is an elegantly dressed, much bejewelled lady. Her epi- 35
taph is carved in a large 'classical' script on the lower edge of the casket:

seianti hanunia tlesnasa

The first letter of the family name (Hanunia), because of its rounded form Θ, looks like a *theta;* it is in fact a ⊟. The existence of six other inscriptions naming *velia seianti hanunia* or *senti hanunia* (without a first name), all from Chiusi and vicinity, make it clear that this was the lady's family name. The skeleton, still inside the sarcophagus, was analysed in 1989, revealing that the deceased woman was at least 80 years old.

Much more characteristic of Chiusi than such large, expensive sarcophagi are the cheaper stone or terracotta ash urns for cremation burials. One in the British Museum gives a good idea of the brightly coloured relief decoration which once ornamented them.

35 Terracotta sarcophagus of Seianti Hanunia Tlesnasa, from Chiusi, *c.*150 BC. H.122 cm, L.183 cm (Terracotta D786, 1887.4–2.1; *CIE* 1454).

cover The casket shows a battle between warriors. The figure of the deceased, reclining as usual on the lid, holds a patera with which to offer a libation to the gods. He wears a costume appropriate for a high rank in a Roman context: the vertical purple stripe of his *chiton* or tunic and deep red border of the toga, whose rounded edge is displayed just below the waist, and a gold ring, worn only by someone with the rank of knight or higher.

The casket bears an epitaph painted in brown along the upper border:

thana ancarui thelesa, 'Thana Ancarui Thelesa'.

The lower part of the 𐌓 is erased; earlier scholars read the name as 'Ancapui,' 𐌀𐌍𐌂𐌀𐌐𐌖𐌉. But while the family name 'Ancapui' does not occur, the name 'Ancarui' recurs several times at Chiusi and Tarquinia. Although the figure on the lid is male, the name on the casket is that of a woman. Lids and caskets were often exchanged between the time of their discovery and their sale and final placement in museums. Perhaps, however, the heirs originally purchased an urn which was readily available, though it represented a man rather than a woman, and had it inscribed with the name of the deceased.

A sarcophagus of a member of the Vipinana family, from near Tuscania and now in the
36 British Museum, has the following inscription:

(1) (2) (3) (4) (5) (6) (7) (8)
vipinans śethre velthur[u]s meclasial thanchvilu avils cis cealchs

'Vipinans Sethre, [son of] Velthur [and of the daughter of] Meclas, Thanchvilu, [lived] years three-and-thirty.'

36 Stone sarcophagus of Sethre Vipinans from Tuscania, with the image of the deceased reclining on the lid. Hellanistic. H.60 cm, L.201 cm, W.64 cm (BM D31–2, 1838.6–8.4; *TLE* 180, *CIE* 5702). Below: Drawing of inscription.

We have here (1) the family name, Vipinans; (2) the first name, Sethre; (3) the patronymic, Velthur; the matronymic, including (4) the mother's family name, Meclasia, and (5) the mother's first name, Thanchvilu.

The word *avil* ('year') occurs more than a hundred times in funerary inscriptions. It is found with the single stem (*avil*) when used with the verbs *svalce* or *svalthas* ('to live'). When used with *lupu* ('dead'), we find *avils,* perhaps a dative of 'time when'. Evidently *avil* indicates a continuous action, 'he lived for X years . . .', while *avils* expresses a precise action or occurrence, 'he died in such-and-such a year'. The following two inscriptions illustrate the difference:

velthur larisal clan cuclnial thanchvilus lupu avils XXV
'Velthur, the son of Laris [and of] Thanchvil Cuclni, died at 25 years' (on a sarcophagus from Tarquinia).

atnas vel larthal clan svalce avil ↑*XIII zi[la]th maruchva tarils cepta phechucu*
'Atnas Vel, son of Larth, lived years 63, [he was] *zilath maruchva* (a magistrate) . . .' 37
(the translation of *tarils cepta phechucu* is uncertain).

This inscription is on a sarcophagus from near Tuscania.

37 Stone (*nenfro*) sarcophagus of Vel Atna, with relief decoration showing a procession of magistrates. From Tuscania, *c.*250–200 BC. H.62 cm, L.213 cm, W.64 cm (BM D26, 1838.6-8.24; *TLE* 194, *CIE* 5755). Below: Drawing of inscription.

Another inscription in the British Museum, on an urn from Volterra, illustrates a different way of expressing age at death (for abbreviations of names, see Appendix I):

ls. cala. ls. ril. ↑*XX*
'Lars Cala, son of Lars, at the age of LXX', i.e. 'Lars Cala, son of Lars, [died] at the age of 70 years.'

Votive figures

Among the rare Etruscan objects found in non-funerary contexts are votive gifts. The inscriptions on these objects document the offerings people made to the gods, giving us a glimpse into their public and private religion, the divinities they worshipped and the gifts considered appropriate. Sometimes ambitious votive offerings, like the Chimaera of Arezzo, may have been made by a whole community. Inscribed on these gifts were the names of the individuals offering them and the names of the divinities to whom they were dedicated as a form of worship or cult. These were sometimes identified with Greek gods and therefore bear the names of Artemis (Aritimi), Minerva (Menrva), etc.; but in fact these gifts were deposited in the sanctuaries of local divinities. Many votive objects – where we know their actual provenance – come from the central Etruscan area around Lake Bolsena: Bolsena, Chiusi, Perugia, etc. This was a region of sanctuaries: as we have seen, the longest ritual inscriptions come from there.

From sanctuaries in Southern Etruria (Veii, Cerveteri, Pyrgi, Gravisca), Latium and Campania (Lavinium, Capua, Paestum), Magna Graecia and Sicily, come thousands of terracotta votive figures – models of eyes, uteri, breasts, genitals, feet and hands – as well as images of *kourotrophoi* (mothers and children) and other inexpensive votive figures asking favours or giving thanks for the health and protection of the faithful or for the birth and well-being of children. Such terracotta votive offerings came from a poorer class of people and were not identified with names. In contrast, more expensive gifts, bronze statuettes, incense burners, etc., proudly record the names of the rich donor and the divinity to whom the gift was offered. Two handsome bronze statuettes in the British Museum, in the late Classical style (about 400–350 BC) bear such inscriptions. Both are solid cast, both represent youths with short hair and both are dedicated to the god Selvans (Silvanus). One youth wears a mantle with rounded borders – the Etruscan *tebenna*, 38

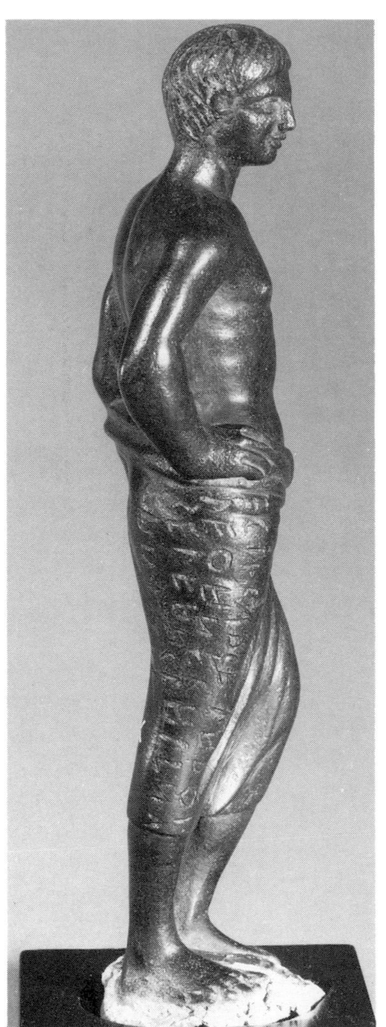

38 Bronze statuette of a youth wearing a short mantle, dedicated to the god Selvans, 400–350 BC. H.16.2 cm (BM Br 678, 1824.4-97.3; *TLE* 559, *CIE* 2403).

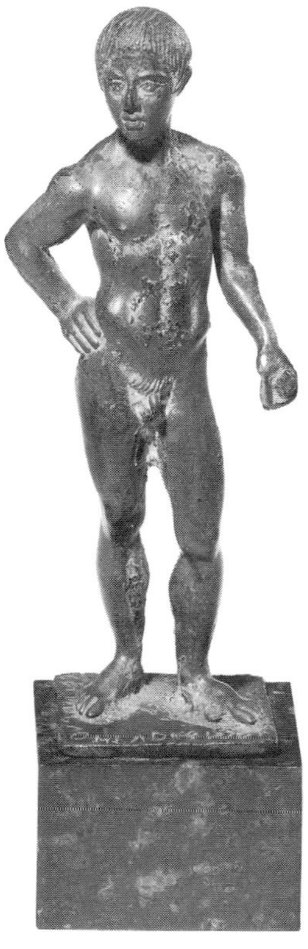

39 Bronze statuette of a naked athlete, dedicated to the god Selvans. From Sarteano (Chiusi), *c*.400–350 BC. H.15.6 cm (BM Br 611, 1865.7–12.12; *TLE* 504). *Below* Detail of inscription.

antecedent of the Roman toga. On the mantle, along the right leg, runs the inscription:

> *ecn turce larthi lethanei alpnu selvansl canzate*
> 'This gave Larthi Lethanei as a gift to Selvans Canzate.'

Ecn, 'this', is the accusative of *eca, ika*. *Turce*, 'gave, dedicated', is the later (neo-Etruscan) form of the Archaic *turuce*. *Ecn turce* is the standard formula for the beginning of votive inscriptions in neo-Etruscan. *Alpnu* here seems to function as the direct object of *turce* (though scholars usually translate the word as 'gladly, willingly'). The donor was a woman: Larthi Lethanei. *Canzate*, an unknown word, seems to be a epithet of Selvans, perhaps referring to a particular region or cult-centre where he was worshipped.

The other bronze statuette, from Sarteano, near Chiusi, represents a naked youth in the Greek manner. The *kouros*, or handsome naked athlete, belongs to a Greek tradition 39
beginning perhaps as early as 700 BC. Etruscans followed the artistic tradition, and at times the athletic custom as well. The dedication is incised into the flat rectangular base, cast in one piece with the statuette:

> *vel śapu th/n turke śel/van/ś[. . .]ran*, or, more probably: *selvanś [. . .]ran)*
> 'Vel Sapu this gave to Selvans [. . .]ran.'

Thn is a variant of *ecn*, 'this'. This statuette was dedicated by a man, Vel Sapu; the epithet of Selvans ([. . .]*ran*) is unfortunately illegible. Both inscriptions seem to have Selvans in the genitive, but formed in different ways. One has the genitive suffix *-l*; in the other, nothing is added to the *-s* of the nominative to form the genitive *-ś* ending.

The importance of the god Selvans in Etruria is proved by the appearance of his name on the Piacenza liver (twice). It also appears on a significant group of ten dedications, eight of which are on bronze statuettes. One (from Tarquinia, now in the Vatican Museum) represents a baby wearing a good-luck charm, or *bulla*. The others, including two in the British Museum, show young men, either bare-chested with low-slung cloaks or nude. Three were dedicated by women (Larthi Lethanei, Velusa [. . .]ans, and Ramtha Uftatavi, the latter perhaps meant to be Uftavi: compare Latin Octavius).

One of these statuettes, in a private collection, is noteworthy for its unique inscription. Incised in vertical lines, it is scratched into the surface, starting from the right underarm. The words are divided by two dots:

> *ecn: turce: avle: havrnas: tuthina: apana: selvansl: tularis*
> 'This gave Aule Havrna, a votive gift (?), on behalf of his father, to Selvans of the Boundaries.'

Avle is the neo-Etruscan form of the Archaic Avile. In a parallel development, the form *Havrna* is related to the name Havrenie on the bronze wine service from Bolsena. The statuette also probably comes from Bolsena, where Havrenie (Havrna) was evidently an important name. *Apana,* 'paternal', agrees with a recently discovered inscription which refers to *apa atic,* 'father (*apa*) and mother (*ati*)'. The translation of *tuthina* here poses a problem; according to one scholar it means 'votive object'. But on the mantle of the famous life-size bronze Orator ('Arringatore') in Florence it has been translated as 'people'.

Coins

40 Etruscan coins, with their legends and symbols, give us a glimpse into another aspect of the life of these ancient and wealthy cities. The legends, like the designs, are in relief.

On the coin in Fig. 40b, *pupluna* identifies the city of origin as Populonia, whose coins have come down to us in great numbers. Also known as Fufluna, Pupluna is the city of Fufluns (just as Athens is the city of Athena). Many coins come from Volsinii (Velznani, abbreviated Velz): a unique gold piece is in the British Museum. Volsinii was so wealthy that when the Romans sacked it they carried off two thousand bronze statues.

The legend *thezl,* or *thezi,* on some beautiful silver coins, cannot be related to any city we know.

We also find the following marks of value on Etruscan coins.

⋊	= 100	>IIX	= 12½
↑	= 50	X	= 10
XXX	= 30	Λ	= 5
ΛXX	= 25	<II	= 2
XX	= 20	I	= 1

a. Silver stater of Thezle, uncertain mint, 4th century BC. Unique. 9.26 g. Obverse: three-quarter head of bull; around it, the inscription *thezle*. Reverse: swimming hippocamp (BM PCG III.C3.901315–4; *TLE* 786).

b. Bronze sextans of Populonia, 3rd century BC. 12.4 g. Obverse: head of Herakles. Reverse: bow, arrow and club with inscription below, *pupluna*; between the arrow and the club a mark of value: two pellets (BMC Populonia, Appendix 3; *TLE* 789).

c. Gold stater of Volsinii, *c.*300 BC. Unique. 4.67 g. Obverse: laureate young male head; below, on either side, a mark of value: X X. Reverse: a bull, with a dove flying above and a star; below, the inscription *Velznani* (BM PCG III.C2, 1848.8–19.1).

40 Silver, bronze and gold coins, inscribed Thezle, Pupluna, Velznani.

5
Etruscan Inscriptions as Historical Evidence

Inscriptions give evidence, direct and indirect, about Etruscan history, illuminating events and personages otherwise known to us only through the accounts of Greek and Roman authors. They testify to cultural, commercial and political contacts; and provide evidence about Etruscan society, religion, customs, magistracies and, through the mythological names, both local and those adapted from the Greeks, faint glimpses of the possible subjects of Etruscan literature and drama.

The gold tablets from Pyrgi record, around 500 BC, an historical event – the dedication of a cult place by Thefarie Velianas, king of Caere, to Phoenician Astarte (Ishtar, identified with Uni: Roman Juno) – and are consistent with the close alliance between Etruscans and Carthaginians mentioned by Aristotle in the fourth century. Just the names bring us closer to this historical past: Thefarie Velianas' first name would have been Tiberius in Latin. The ancient name of one of Caere's ports was Punicum, no doubt because of the intense traffic which at one time took place with Phoenician Carthage, whose citizens the Romans called Poeni. At the important sanctuary of Gravisca, the port city of Tarquinia, inhabited by Greeks from 600 to about 480 BC, gifts were offered and 'signed' by Eudemos (from Athens?); Paktyes, probably a Lydian; Ombrikos, perhaps a Hellenised Umbrian; and, most famous of all, Sostratos of Aegina, who dedicated a marble anchor to Apollo. This Sostratos was probably the same as the merchant mentioned by Herodotus (IV: 152) as trading with Tartessos in Spain.

Other names from inscriptions ring a bell that sounds across the centuries. The name of Hannibal, Rome's great enemy, appears on the epitaph of a certain Felsnas, son of Larth Lethe, who was buried at Tarquinia aged 106 years, and claimed to have fought at Capua during the war with Hannibal (*hanipaluscle*) at the end of the third century BC.

That the Vipinas brothers – pictured on an Etruscan mirror as well as in the wall-paintings of the François Tomb from Vulci, and mentioned in Roman traditions referring to the legendary period of their history in the sixth century BC – were real people is confirmed by a dedication scratched on bucchero vases of the same century from Veii: *avile vipiiennas,* Aulus Vipinas. The wall-paintings of the fourth-century François Tomb also record the names of other characters from Roman history: not only Aule and Caile Vipinas, but also Macstrna (Latin Mastarna, perhaps a title: *magister*?), elsewhere identified as Servius Tullius, Tarquin's heir and king of Rome, and Cneve Tarchunies Rumach, better known to us as Tarquin of Rome. In this 'historical' painting the killing of Tarquin accompanies a surprise attack on Etruscan allies of Rome by a group of heroes from Vulci. The victims came from Volsinii (*velznach*), Sovana (*sveamach*), Rome (*rumach*), and perhaps Falerii.

We have seen that most of the longest Etruscan texts which survive are religious or ritual in character: the Zagreb mummy wrappings, the Capua tile, the lead strip from Santa Marinella, the lead sheet from Magliano and the bronze model of a sheep's liver from Piacenza. This situation confirms the ancients' view of the Etruscans as a deeply religious people. They also wrote books on religion, recorded by Roman writers, which have not survived or been passed on through later copying.

We owe our knowledge of the Etruscans' religious reputation in antiquity to the fact that the Romans admired and adopted many Etruscan rites, rituals and traditions. They called in Etruscan *haruspices* (priests specialised in divination), and for a while young Roman aristocrats were sent to Etruria, as they were later sent to Athens, to complete their education (Livy IX. 36). These young aristocrats evidently learned in Etruria the art of reading signs and omens, essential for generals, who had to observe such signs and prudently interrogate the gods about their intentions before setting off on a campaign.

In the ancient Mediterranean, in Italy, in Rome and the Etruscan cities, where many gods held court, it was of the utmost importance to know precisely which god was involved in a particular affair. The divisions marked on the Piacenza liver reflected the regions of the sky and their boundaries, making it possible for the faithful to address their prayers, and their gifts, to the right god. Only thus could religious rites and prayers be effective. Ritual calendars like that on the Zagreb mummy wrappings specified which sacrifices and offerings were to be made to a particular god on a specific day. Votive offerings bore the name of the donor and that of the divinity as a reminder to the god.

Writing had a special significance then which it no longer has today: it was powerful magic. When you wrote down a name you acted on it, for good or bad. You gave it a force and a permanence far beyond that of the spoken word. A prayer, or a curse, was written down in order to make if efficacious, so that it would *work*. In the same way, centuries later, Scandinavian runes (themselves derived from Etruscan script) were incised on spears to ensure that they hit their mark.

Just as many inscriptions and public monuments in Athens, informing the people of even minor events and expenses, testify to the reality of fifth-century democracy, so Etruscan epitaphs testify to the prestige of their noble families, while the religious inscriptions of the Etruscan cities testify to the importance of their religious rites and to their ideas of the importance of boundaries (*tular*) of space – regions of land and sky, places between the living and the dead – and of time, the *saecula*. These boundaries were marked in many ways. Epitaphs, or *elogia,* the praise of the dead, funeral ceremonies, memorial services: these all had a special importance because the Etruscans had a special regard for the family dead. This is borne out by the richly furnished tombs and the many representations of male and female figures which, once thought to be wholly divine or wholly human, are now better understood as representing images of ancestors – the 'heroised' dead. For an aristocratic family, the family tomb was a central symbol. So was the genealogy of the deceased, including the mother's family, and the visual reminder of their life, their marriage, their journey to the Underworld, the Greek mythology which bore witness to their culture. Later, when the 'middle class' family emerged, it adopted
the symbols and insignia of the élite. The family tombs of Volterra, Perugia, Chiusi, 41
Tarquinia and other cities were filled with ash chests and caskets bearing images of the deceased, epitaphs and representations of Greek myths. Even the cheapest burials – as, in Chiusi, terracotta *ollae* or vases containing the ashes of the dead – were painted or incised with the names of the deceased. When Pallottino called the Etruscans the 'People of the Book', he was calling attention to this ritual aspect of writing.

The number of surviving mirrors, their beauty and the interest of their scenes, often labelled with inscriptions, testify to the literacy, culture and wealth of the Etruscan women for whom they were made. The importance of women in religion is shown for example by the fact that three out of ten surviving dedications to the god Selvans (p. 48) were made by women (though it could be that Selvans was in fact more closely associated with women). From the very earliest periods women received burials as luxurious as those of men – we have seen several of these in the preceding pages – and in general were held in high esteem in aristocratic Etruscan society.

The importance of the woman's family is shown by the use of matronymics in many epitaphs. Yet Etruscan society was not matriarchal, as Bachofen believed (*Tanaquil*, 1870). Matronymics in fact occur less often than patronymics and are regularly placed after them. We do not even know the word for 'husband': we only know the name of the 'wife (*puia*) of so-and-so'; not 'so-and-so's husband'.

We know the names of many Etruscan magistracies and priesthoods which lasted as long as the Etruscan cities maintained their independence and their language. Prayers and magic spells in the Etruscan language survived beyond, into the Roman world, as exotic remnants. This was a world that spoke and wrote Latin and Greek, but on which the Etruscans had left their mark; and one which we cannot understand without taking into account what they have left behind, their monuments, their traditions and their inscriptions.

41 Red-figure crater from Vulci, *c.*350 BC, with Aivas (Ajax), despondent at his failure to win the arms of Achilles, committing suicide by impaling himself on his sword. His name is painted above, in white. H.39.75 cm (BM Vase F480, 1867.5–8.1328).

6
Oscan: The Agnone Tablet

The Italic branch of the Indo-European family of languages consists of Latin, Umbrian, the dialects of the central Italian mountain tribes – the Marsi, Marrucini, etc. – and Oscan. The Oscan language coincides with the territory inhabited by the Samnite tribes: inscriptions have been found in Samnium, Campania, Apulia, Lucania and Bruttium, but most come from Pompeii and Capua. The earliest are coin legends of about 400 BC; the latest, graffiti from the walls of Pompeii, probably dating from the early years of the first century BC. Over 200 inscriptions survive. Indeed, Oscan was not an unimportant dialect: after Etruscan, it was the chief language of central Italy, while Latin was limited to Rome and Latium.

Three alphabets were used: Oscan, Greek and Latin. The Oscan alphabet was usually 42
written with finely traced letters. A reform of the writing system, in about 300 BC, added the letters 𐌞 and 𐌟, transcribed as *í* and *ú,* to signify the long vowels. *U* was used – often but not always – for *o*. Characteristic is the A, 𐌀 in its latest form. The *d* is written as *R* (the letter the Latins regularly used for the sound of *r*). There was thus an exchange of signs, since the sound of *r* was indicated by the letter *D*. Digamma (𐌅), pronounced like Latin *v* or English *w*), must have been semi-vocalic, since it often appears in diphthongs: for example, *thesavrum,* Latin *thesaurus,* Greek *thesaurós. Z* was pronounced (as in Etruscan) *t* + *s*. *I* was used to express an original *e: íst* = Latin *est*. The existence of the letter 8, pronounced *f,* was, in Oscan as in Umbrian, due to direct Etruscan influence. A Greek model, parallel to the Etruscan model, would account for the letters for *b, g* and *d* (*B, G* and *R*), which are absent or transformed in Etruscan: the reintroduction of the sounds *b, g, d* and the corresponding letters *B, G* and *R* resulted from contacts with the cities of Magna Graecia.

Apart from the Oscan alphabet, a Greek alphabet (Ionic-Tarentine) prevailed, not surprisingly, in the regions of Magna Graecia, in Lucania and Bruttium, as well as among the Mamertines in Sicily. Later the Latin alphabet was used in colonies: the Oscan Tavola Bantina, for example, is written in this alphabet. For a number of years the Greek alphabet, which was long-lived, overlapped with the use of the Latin.

Though we derive most of what we know about Oscan from inscriptions, certain observations on peculiarities of the language by ancient scholars, such as Varro (first century BC), have come down to us. These ancient scholars recognised Oscan, like Etruscan, as a distinct, separate language. We are told that Latin *quidquid,* 'whatever', was equivalent in pronunciation to Oscan *pitpit;* this means that the sound *kw* was rendered as a *p*. Varro also tells us (*Lingua Latina,* VII:29), '*senem . . . Osci casnar appellant*', 'the Oscans call an old man *casnar*'.

Oscan, Umbrian, Latin, and the other Indo-European dialects of central Italy were spoken by neighbouring peoples for a considerable length of time, and influenced each other. But Oscan shows surprisingly close similarities with languages other than Latin, particularly with Greek and with the Germanic languages. For example, the word for

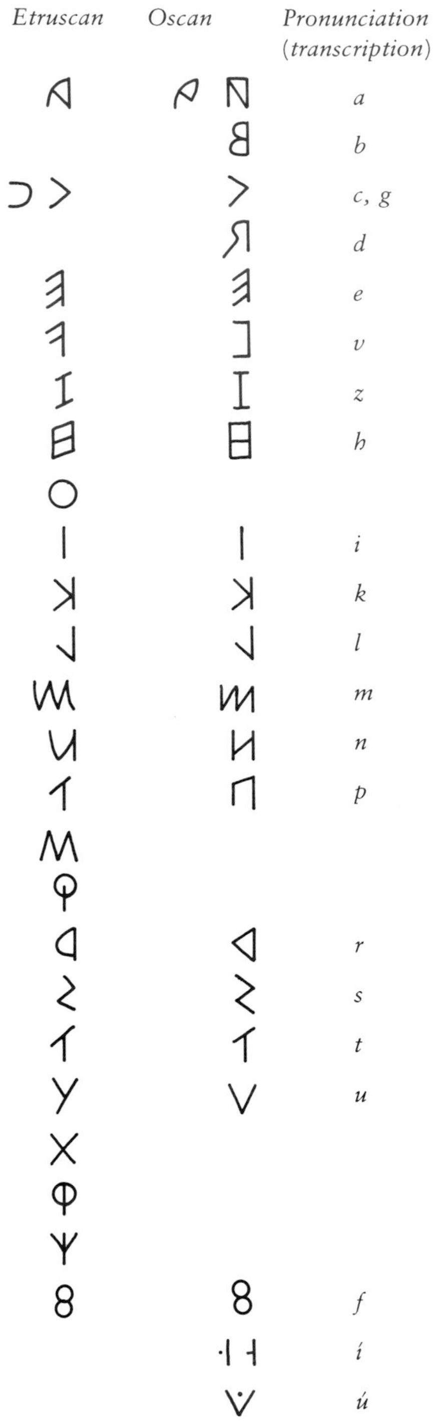

Etruscan	Oscan	Pronunciation (transcription)
𐌀	𐌀 𐌀	*a*
	𐌁	*b*
𐌂 𐌂	𐌂	*c, g*
	𐌃	*d*
𐌄	𐌄	*e*
𐌅	𐌅	*v*
𐌆	𐌆	*z*
𐌇	𐌇	*h*
𐌈		
𐌉	𐌉	*i*
𐌊	𐌊	*k*
𐌋	𐌋	*l*
𐌌	𐌌	*m*
𐌍	𐌍	*n*
𐌐	𐌐	*p*
𐌑		
𐌒		
𐌓	𐌓	*r*
𐌔	𐌔	*s*
𐌕	𐌕	*t*
𐌖	𐌖	*u*
𐌗		
𐌘		
𐌙		
𐌚	𐌚	*f*
	𐌝	*í*
	𐌞	*ú*

42 Etruscan and Oscan alphabets.

'daughter' in Oscan is *futreí,* related to German *tochter,* English *daughter,* Greek *thugater*; in contrast, the Latin word *filia* is quite unrelated to Oscan.

The Romans did not pressure their neighbours to change over to Latin. The allies of Rome eventually felt it would be to their advantage to adopt the more prestigious Roman language: in 180 BC Cumae asked the Roman Senate for permission to adopt Latin as their official language instead of Oscan. For a long time, however, Oscan continued to be spoken and written in Pompeii and elsewhere as the unofficial but real language of the people.

The principal Oscan inscriptions are the Tavola Bantina, written in Latin characters; the *cippus* from Abella; the tablet from Agnone; and groups of ritual inscriptions known as the *iúvilas* and *eítuns,* from the appearance of these words in the texts. In addition to ritual, votive, commemorative and funerary texts, we have building inscriptions and magical inscriptions.

The famous bronze tablet from Agnone, 43
in Samnite country (Molise), was discovered in 1848. Measuring 28 × 16.5 cm, the tablet has a handle, with an iron chain from which it could be hung. It is said to have been found in a sanctuary, some traces of which still survive. It has been variously dated: some consider it the oldest Oscan inscription (*c.* 250 BC), others date it somewhat later. Inscribed on both sides are the directions on the route to follow during the course of a ritual ceremony. The list of 'stations' inside and outside the *húrtín*

keriiín, the 'garden, or enclosure, of Ceres', has been compared to the Christian ritual of the Stations of the Cross. Such a topographic route consists of separate 'stations' (*statíf*), each of which has a special significance, or is evocative of a particular event. In the case of the Oscan ritual, each refers to the altar of a particular divinity, which is mentioned at some length on side A, and listed again more summarily on side B. To be noted is the close relationship of the back and front of the tablet, with each divinity's 'station' lined up front and back.

Some scholars have interpreted *statíf* as 'statue' or 'construction', rather than 'station'. It seems clear, in any case, that it coincides with the placement of the altar (*aasa*) of each god. These are all divinities connected with agriculture. They belong to the circle of Ceres, or Demeter, and in some cases show the influence of Magna Graecia; we can compare, for example, the ritual on the Etruscan inscription from Capua, not too far from this area.

43 Bronze tablet from Agnone, *c.*250 BC, inscribed front and back (BM Br 888, 1873.8–20.119).

Side A

1. *statús. pús. set. húrtín.* | *kerriiín.* 2. *vezkeí. statíf.* 3. *evklúí. statíf. kerrí. statíf.* 4. *futreí. kerríiaí. státíf.* 5. *anter. stataí. statíf.* 6. *ammaí. kerríiaí. statíf.* 7. *diumpaís. kerríiaís. statíf.* 8. *líganakdíkeí. entraí. statíf.* 9. *anafriss. kerríiúís. statíf.* 10. *maatúís. kerríiúís. statíf.* 11. *diúveí. verehasiúí. statíf.* 12. *diúveí. regatureí. statíf.* 13. *hereklúí. kerríiúí. statíf.* 14. *patanaí. piístíaí. statíf.* 15. *deívaí. genetaí. statíf.* 16. *aasaí. purasiaí.* 17. *saahtúm. tefúrúm. alttreí.* 18. *pútereípíd. akeneí.* 19. *sakahíter.* 20. *fiuusasiaís. az. húrtúm.* 21. *sakarater.* 22. *pernaí. kerríiaí. statíf.* 23. *ammaí. kerríiaí. statíf.* 24. *fluusaí. kerríiaí. statíf.* 25. *evklúí. patereí. statíf.*

Latin translation

1. Ritus qui sunt in horto Cereali 2.*Vensici statio 3. Euclo statio. Cereri statio 4. Filiae Cereali statio 5.*Interstitae statio 6. Ammae Cereali statio 7. Lumpis Cerealibus statio 8. Liganacdici *Interae statio 9. Imbribus Cerealibus statio 10. Matis Cerealibus statio 11. Iovi Iuvenali statio 12. Iovi Rectori statio 13. Herculi Cereali statio 14. Patanae Pistiae statio 15. Divae Genitae statio 16–19. In ara igniaria sanctum holocaustum altero quoque anno sanciatur 20. Floralibus ad hortum sacratur 21. Pernae Cereali statio 22. Ammae Cereali statio 24. Florae Cereali statio 25. Euclo patri statio

English translation

1. The established ritual places which are in the enclosure of Ceres; 2. The stopping-place for Vensicus; 3. The stopping-place for Euclus; the stopping-place for Ceres; 4. The stopping-place for Ceres' Daughter; 5. The stopping-place for Interstita; 6. The stopping-place for Amma; 7. The stopping-place for the Nymphs of Ceres; 8. The stopping-place for Liganacdix Interna 9. The stopping-place for the Rains of Ceres; 10. The stopping-place for the Matis of Ceres; 11. The stopping-place for Jupiter Juvenal; 12. The stopping-place for Jupiter Rector, or Irrigator; 13. The stopping-place for Hercules of Ceres; 14. The stopping-place for Patana Pistis; 15. The stopping-place for the Goddess Genita. 16–19. At the Altar of Fire let a holy burnt offering (sacrifice) be sanctified every other year; 20–21. To the Florae by the enclosure let there be a sacrifice; 22. The stopping-place for Perna of Ceres; 23. The stopping-place for Amma of Ceres; 24. The stopping-place for Flora of Ceres; 25. The stopping-place for Euclus the Father.

Side B

1. *aasas. ekask. eestínt.* 2. *húrtúí.* 3. *vezkeí.* 4. *evklúí.* 5. *fuutreí.* 6. *anter. stataí.* 7. *kerrí.* 8. *ammaí.* 9. *diumpaís.* 10. *líganakdíkeí. entraí.* 11. *kerríiaí.* 12. *anafriss.* 13. *maatúís.* 14. *diúveí. verehasiú.* 15. *diúveí. piíhiúí. regatureí.* 16. *hereklúí. kerríiúí.* 17. *patanaí. piístíaí.* 18. *deívaí. genetaí.* 19. *aasaí. purasiaí.* 20. *saahtúm. tefúrúm.* 21. *alttreí. pútereípíd.* 22. *akeneí.* 23. *húrz. dekmanniúís. staít.*

Latin translation

1–2. Arae hae extant | horto 3.*Vensici 4. Euclo 5. Filiae 6. Interstitae 7. Cereri 8. Ammae 9. Lumpis 10. Liganacdici Interae 11. Cereali 12. Imbribus 13. Matis 14. Iovi Iuvenali 15. Iovi Pio Rectori 16. Herculi Cereali 17. Patanae Pistiae 18. Divae Genitae 19. In ara igniaria 20–21. sanctum holocaustum altero quoque anno 23. hortus pensionibus decimanis stat.

English translation

1–2. These altars stand in the enclosure: 3. for Vensicus; 4. for Euclus; 5. for the Daughter; 6. for Interstita; 7. for Ceres; 8. for Amma; 9. for the Nymphs; 10–11. for Liganacdica Interna of Ceres; 12. for the Rains; 13. for the Matis; 14. for Jupiter Juvenalis; 15. for Jupiter Pius Rector; 16. for Heracles of Ceres; 17. for Patina Pistia; 18. for Divine Genita; 19. At the Altar of Fire 20. a holy burnt offering 21–22. every other year. 23. The enclosure is at the disposal of the Decimani.

Notes

Side A

2. *Vensicus:* uncertain. Related to Venus?
3. Greek *Euklos,* a chthonic divinity, of the circle of Demeter.
4. Ceres' Daughter = Persephone, Proserpina.
5. 'The Goddess Between' (the mother and the daughter?).
6, 23. *Amma*: 'mummy', mother
7. Nymphs: divinities of the springs
8. *Legifera* = Lawgiver? Latin *lex,* Oscan *ligud; Interna* = in between Nymphs, that is water of the earth, and rain, water from the sky = perhaps the dew.
10. *Matis*, perhaps related to Mater Matuta, or an Italic divinity; related to *maturus* = 'ripe'?
13. Hercules is not usually involved with Ceres, earth divinities or vegetation; but in the Roman world he is sometimes connected with Silvanus (Etruscan *Selvans*).
14. *Patana* = *Panda* in Latin, goddess of opening, ripening plants. The epithet *Pistis* is related to either faith or threshing.
15. *Genita:* birth of plants.
16. *Aasai purasiaí;* compare Latin *ara,* 'altar'; Greek πῦρ, 'fire'.
17. *Saahtúm tefúrún:* 'a sacrifice with fire'; *tefúrún* is probably connected with Greek τέφρα, 'cinders', 'ashes'. 20. *Fiuusasiasís:* compare Latin *Flora,* Italian *fiore.* 25. *Patereí:* 'father'.

Side B

1. *aasas ekask:* the altars of the *hortus,* dedicated to the individual divinities. *eestínt:* elsewhere *stahínt.*
23. *húrz dekmanniúís staít:* ceremonies in the *hortus,* where the offering of the tithe was carried out. The *Dekmannis* was apparently the priesthood in charge of performing these rites in the enclosure.

APPENDIX 1
Etruscan Names

PRAENOMINA (First Names)

Abbreviations

MASCULINE

A, Ar, Ath	Arnth, Aranth = Latin Arruns
Au, Av	Aule, Avle, Avile = Latin Aulus
C, Ca	Cae, Cai = Latin Caius, Gaius
V, Ve, Vl	Vel
Vth	Velthur
Lc	Larce
L, La, Lth	Larth
L, Li, Lr	Laris, Lars
M	Marce = Latin Marcus
S, Sth	Sethre
Ti	Tite = Latin Titus

FEMININE

H, Ha, F, Fa	Hasti(a), Fasti(a)
Th, Tha	Thana
Thch	Thanchvil = Latin Tanaquil (*thana* + *cvil* = 'gift of Thana'?)
R, Ra	Ramtha
Rav, Rn	Ra(v)ntha, Raunthu

Other first names

MASCULINE	FEMININE
Cneve = Latin Cnaeus, Gnaeus	Sethra
Caile = Latin Caelus	Velia
Cuinte = Latin Quintus	Larthi(a)
Spurie = Latin Spurius	Arnthi
Mamarce	Tita
Thefarie = Latin Tiberius	

APPENDIX 2
Glossary of Etruscan Words

*Words preceded by an asterisk are reconstructed from forms given by Greek and Roman writers. For names of divinities, see Index. For further information see vocabulary lists in Pallottino, *Etruscans*; Pfiffig, *Etruskische Sprache*; and *Thesaurus*.

A 𐌀

ac make, offer, act; *acazr* objects offered in the tomb
acale (*Aclus*) June
ais, eis (pl. *aisar, eisar*) god
aisiu divine, of the gods
aisna, eisna divine, of the gods
al give, offer
alpan, alpnu gift, offering; willingly
alphaze offering
alumnathe sacred society
am to be
an (*ana, ane, anc, ananc*) he, she
apa father
apana paternal
apcar abacus
ar-, er- to make, move, build
**arac* falcon
**arim* monkey
ars- push away?
aska type of vase (Gk *askós*)
athre building (Lat. *atrium*?)
ati, ativu mother, 'mummy'
ati nacna grandmother
avil year

C 𐌂) 𐌊

-c and
ca this
camthi name of a magistracy
cape, capi vase, container (cf Lat. *capiō*?)
**capr-* April
capra urn
**capu* falcon
car-, cer- make, build
cecha sacred things, ritual, ceremony, priestly; *zilch cechaneri* a title (see *zil* etc.)
cechase name of magistracy
cehen this one here
cela room (Lat. *cella*)
celi September
celu priestly title
cep-, cepen priestly title
ces- lie
cezp 8?
cezpalch 80?
ci 3
cialch-, cealch- 30
ciz three times
cisra Caere
clan (pl. *clenar*) son
cletram basin, basket, cart for offerings (Umbrian *kletra*)
cleva offering
clevsin Chiusi
creal magistrate
creice Greek (Lat. *Graecus*)
culichna vase, 'little kylix' (Gk *kylix*)
cupe cup (Gk *kúpē*, Lat. *cupa*)
cver, cvil gift, offering

Ch 𐌙

**chosfer* (gloss) October

E ꟻ

eca (see *ca*)
eleivana of oil; *aska eleivana* vessel for oil (Gk *élaion*)
-em minus
enac, *enach* then, afterwards
epl, *pi*, *pul* in, to, up to
eslz twice
etera, *eteri* foreigner; slave, client (serf?)
etnam and, also

F 8

**falatu* (gloss, *falado*) sky
fan- to consecrate?
fanu sacred place (Lat. *fānum*?)
favi grave, temple vault (Lat. *fauissa*?)
fler offering, sacrifice
flerchva all the statues, offerings
flere divinity, god
flereś statue
frontac interpreter of lightning; see *trutnuth* (Gk. *brontē*?)
fufluna see *pupluna*

H 日⊘

hanthin in front of
hec-, *hech-* put, place in front of, add
herma, *heramasva* place, statue? (Gk Hermes)
herme, *hermu* sacred society of Hermes
**hermi-* (gloss, *Ermius*) August
hinthial soul, ghost, reflection
hintha, hinthu, hinththin below
hus- (pl. *husiur*) youth, children; *huzrnatre* group of youths
huth 6

I |

ic, *ich*, *ichnac* how
ica, *ika* this
ilu- verb of offering or prayer
in, *inc* it
ipa relative pronoun
ipe, ipa whoever, whatever
**ister* (gloss: Lat. *histrio*) actor
ita, *itu* this
**itu-* (gloss: *itus* or *ituare*) to divide? (Lat. *Idus*)

L ⅃

lauchum king (Lat. *lucumō*)
lauchumna 'belonging to a *lucumo*' (king or prince), palace
lautni 'of the family', freedman
lautnitha, *lautnita* freedwoman
lautun, *lautn* family, *gens*
lechtum vase for oil (Gk *lēkythos*)
lechtumuza little *lēkythos*
lein- to die?
les- offer sacrifice
leu lion
lucair to rule
luth sacred place
lup-, *lupu* to die

M ⋎ ⩘

-m, *-um* and
mach 5
macstrev name of magistracy
mal- to give, dedicate?
malena, *malstria* mirror
man, *mani* the dead (Lat. *Manes*)
manin- to offer to the Manes?
maru, *marunu* name of magistracy (Lat. *marō*, Umbr. *maron-*)
masan, *masn* name of month?
matam, *matan* above, before
math honey, honeyed wine
maruchva type of *zilath*
mech people, league
men- offer
methlum district
mi, *mini* I, me
mul- to offer, dedicate as an *ex-voto*
mulach, *malak*, *mlach* votive offering, dedication
mun-, *muni* underground place, tomb

mur- stay, reside
murś urn, sarcophagus
mutana, *mutna* sarcophagus

N 𐌍 𐌍

nac how, as, because
neftś, *nefś*, *nefiś* grandson (Lat. *nepos*)
nene nurse, wet-nurse
neri water
nesna belonging to the dead?
nethśra haruspicina
netśvis haruspex
nuna offering?
nurph- 9

P 𐌐

pachathur Bacchante, maenad
pachie- pachana Bacchic
pacusnaśie, *pacuśnasie* Bacchic, Dionysiac
papa, *papacs* grandfather
papals of the grandfather: grandson
parnich magistrate
patna name of vase (Gk *patane*, Lat. *patina*?)
penthuna, *penthna* cippus, stone?
pi, *pul* at, in, through
pruch, *pruchum* jug (Gk *próchous*)
prumathś, *prumats* great-grandson (Lat. *pronepos*)
puia wife
pul see *pi*
pulumchva stars?
pupluna, *fufluna* Populonia
purth, *purthne* name of magistrate or magistracy; dictator?
put-, *puth-* cup, vase, well? (Lat. *puteus*, *puteal*?)

Q 𐌒

qutun, *qutum* vase (Gk *kōthōn*)

R 𐌓

rach- prepare
**rasenna*, *rasna* Etruscan, of Etruria
rath sacred thing
ratum according to law (Lat. *rite*)
ril aged, at the age of . . . (years)
rumach Roman, from Rome
ruva brother

S, Ś 𐌑 𐌔

(*s* and *ś* are often interchangeable)
śa 4
sac- carring out a sacred act
sacni sanctuary
sacnisa consecrate?
sal- make, carry out
śar, *zar* 10
sath-, *śat-* put, establish, be put?
śealch 40
sec, *sech* daughter
semph 7?
semphalch 70?
slicaches sacred society?
snenath maid, companion (f)
spur- city
spurana, *spureni* having to do with the city
śran, *sren* ornament, figure
srencve decorated with figures?
suc- declare
suplu flutist (Lat. *subulo*)
śuth-, *sut-* to stay, place?
śuthi tomb, grave
śuthina for the tomb, sepulchral gift
sval alive, to live
sve similarly
sveamach from Sovana

T 𐌕 𐌕

ta this
tamera name of magistracy
tarchnalthi at Tarquinia
ten- to act as
tes-, *tesam-* to care for

tesinth caretaker
teta grandmother
tev- to show, set?
tevarath onlooker, judge at the games, umpire
tin- day
tiu, *tiv-*, *tiur* moon, month
tmia place, sacred building
-tnam see *etnam*
trin- to plead, supplicate
truth, *trut* libation
trutnuth, *trutnvt* priest (Lat. *fulguriator*)
tul stone
tular, *tularu* boundaries
tunur one at a time
tur- to give
tura incense
turza offering
tus funerary niche
tusurthir married couple? ('in the double urn'?)
tuthi, *tuti-* community, state (Umbrian *tota*?)
tuthin, *tuthina-* of the state, public
tuthina the people; votive object?

Th ⊙O

thafna cup
tham- to build, found
thapna vase (for offerings?)
thaurch funerary
thaure, *thaura* tomb
thez- to make an offering
thezl, *thezi* name of a city found on Etruscan coins
thi pronoun
thina vase, jar (Lat. *tina*, Gk *dînos*)
thu one
thucte name of month
thui here, now
thuni before
thunz once

U Y V

ulpaia jug (Gk *olpe*)
une then
usil the sun
uslane at noon
ut- carry out, perform

V ꟻ

vacal, *vacil*, *vacl* libation?
**velcitna* (gloss, *Velcitanus*) March
velclthi at Vulci
velsnalthi at Volsinii (*velznani*); *velsnach* from Volsinii
vers- fire (or ladle?)
vinum, *vinm* wine (Lat. *uīnum*)

Z I

zal, *zel-*, *esal-* 2
zanena cup
zar see *sar*
zathrum 20
zeri rite, legal action?
zich- to write, incise
zil- to rule?
zil, *zilac*, *zilc*, *zilach*, *zilath* a magistrate (Lat. *praetor*)
ziv having lived, dead at
ziva the dead, deceased

Further Reading

Etruscan

L. Banti, *The Etruscan Cities and their Culture*, Berkeley and Los Angeles, 1973.

G. Bonfante and L. Bonfante, *The Etruscan Language: An Introduction*, Manchester and New York, 1983; trans. as *Lingua e cultura degli Etruschi*, rev. trans. Rome 1985.

Corpus Inscriptionum Etruscarum (*CIE*), various places, 1873, 1970, 1980, ongoing.

M. Cristofani, 'Recent Advances in Etruscan Epigraphy and Language', in *Italy Before the Romans*, ed. D. and F.R.S. Ridgway, London, New York, San Francisco, 1979, 373–412.

N. de Grummond (ed.), *A Guide to Etruscan Mirrors*, Tallahassee (Florida) 1982.

C. de Simone, *Die griechischen Entlehnungen im Etruskischen*, 2 vols, Wiesbaden 1968–70.

E. Macnamara, *The Etruscans*, London 1990.

E. Macnamara, *Everyday Life of the Etruscans*, London 1973, 172–89.

M. Pallottino, *The Etruscans*, Bloomington (Indiana) and London 1975, 187–234.

M. Pallottino, *Testimonia Linguae Etruscae* (*TLE*), Florence 1968.

A. Pfiffig, *Die etruskische Sprache*, Graz 1969.

E.H. Richardson, 'An Archaeological Introduction to the Etruscan Language', in *Etruscan Life and Afterlife*, ed. L. Bonfante, Detroit, 1986, 215–31.

H. Rix, *Das etruskische Cognomen*, Wiesbaden 1963.

Thesaurus Linguae Etruscae, I, *Indice Lessicale*, Rome 1978.

L.B. van der Meer, *The Bronze Liver of Piacenza*, Amsterdam 1987.

P. Zazoff, *Etruskische Skarabäen*, Mainz 1968.

Oscan

A. Morandi, *Epigrafia Italica*, Rome, 1982, 66, 72, 115–17, 126–30.

V. Pisani, *Le lingue dell'Italia antica oltre il latino*, Turin 1953, 92–5.

A. L. Prosdocimi, 'L'Osco', in *Popoli e civiltà dell'Italia antica* 6, Rome, 1978, 830–38.

Inscriptions Cited but not Illustrated

Page	
12–13	*TLE* 801–58 (glosses)
13	*TLE* 1
15	*TLE* 55
20	cf. *TLE* 504; *TLE* 282
21	*TLE* 399, 278, 282, 1
24–5	*TLE* 156
27	*TLE* 1
28	*TLE* 2, 878, 359 (*CIE* 5237), 570, 131 (*CIE* 5430)
29	*TLE* 719, 752
30	*TLE* 695
34	*TLE* 88, 335
38	de Simone 112–13
39	*TLE* 3, 63, 761, 762, 5, 62, 64; cf. 7–8
41	*TLE* 131 (*CIE* 5430), 190, 174, 902
42–3	BM Br 700, 73.8–20.109 (*CIE* 10875); BM Br 654, 73.8–20.203 (*TLE* 216, *CIE* 10877); BM Br 780, 73.8–20.211 (*TLE* 291–2, *CIE* 10855)
45	*TLE* 129
48	*TLE* 148, 559, 696, 719, 900; 651
50	*TLE* 890, 293–303, 35

Index